Aubrey De Vere

Selections From the Poems of Aubrey de Vere

Aubrey De Vere

**Selections From the Poems of Aubrey de Vere**

ISBN/EAN: 9783744713337

Printed in Europe, USA, Canada, Australia, Japan

Cover: Foto ©Thomas Meinert / pixelio.de

More available books at **www.hansebooks.com**

# SELECTIONS

### FROM THE

## POEMS OF AUBREY DE VERE

Aubrey de Vere

# SELECTIONS

FROM THE

# POEMS OF AUBREY DE VERE

*EDITED WITH A PREFACE*

BY

GEORGE EDWARD WOODBERRY

MACMILLAN AND CO

AND LONDON

1894

Norwood Press:
J. S. Cushing & Co. — Berwick & Smith.
Boston, Mass., U.S.A.

# PREFACE

THE qualities of Aubrey de Vere's poetry are not far to seek. Lyrical in verse, strong in style, mainly historical in theme, heroic or spiritual in substance, above all placid, it stirs and tranquillizes the soul in the presence of lovely scenes, high actions, and those

"Great ideas that man was born to learn;"

and its outlook is upon the field of the soul regenerate, where suffering is remembered only through its purification, blessed in issues of sweetness, dignity, and peace. It takes wide range, but is predominantly either Bardic or Christian. The sympathy of the poet with the ancient Irish spirit must have been fed with patriotic fervour, akin to renewed inspiration, to permit him to render the old lays of his country with such fidelity to their native genius. Cuchullain once more becomes credible to fancy, — the imagination of a childhood world; and the songs of Oiseen and Ethell strike with a music as of anvils. The versions of the three monuments of old Irish story — the "Sorrows of Song" — are our best. The English lines have the definiteness and precision that belong to primitive narrative; and yet each tale is involved in that atmosphere of "the shore of old romance," of the marvellous, the picturesque, the childlike, which appeals to our eyes like the distances of spring — the haze of time lying along the early world. In each of the three mythic poems there are pictures of novel and strange beauty: the boy, Cuchullain, riding laughing home in his car after the deeds of his knighting-day, with the leashed wide-winged birds flying over him, the six leashed stags following the chariot captive, the bandits' heads upon its front; or, the lovers, Naisi and Deirdré, hand in hand on the foot-bridge pouring forth the lay that hemmed them with the clansmen of Usnach; or, King Lir, "with under-sliding arms," by the bed of the gold-woven bridal veil, lifting the children from its dawn-touched glittering tissue to "the first light from the sky." These are such pictures as Burne-Jones is too often thought to have invented.

Of all, Cuchullain is the noblest figure in this old Irish verse; and the poem which relates his deeds — with its episodic tales of his youth, the background of his island-boyhood with the friend he was doomed to slay, and the long duel between them which closes in his lament over the dead man he loved and his retirement to the forest — is so inwrought with bravery, pathos, and emotional beauty as to give it the first place, while the hero's Achillean return to the host places it among true epics. The second of the three "Sorrows"—"The Sons of Usnach"— is characterized by a strange processional beauty, as

of a pageant pilgriming, and by a clear spirit of joyful-
ness in the midst of the moving cloud of fate, like
"the tempest's heart of calm." But the last — "The
Children of Lir" — touches the heart most deeply.
The idea of the poem — the first human effort to ex-
tend the bounds of Divine Mercy, to reach through
the "dark backward and abysm" of the thousand
pagan years, and gather to its fold these children to
be the first-fruits of Christ in their land — is very
noble; but great as is the idea, it is subdued into
a simple idyl of childhood. The poem is, indeed,
unique, and the handling (Tennyson treated it less
admirably) is exquisite. The children in their home
are dear, and in their transformation into swans there
is no discord. The swan-nature, already half-human in
poetic tradition, blends of itself with the ideal image
of childhood; and the nearness of the little exiles to
humanity, after their change, is sustained by their
mystical night-long singing overheard by men, and by
the tale told their poet listening solitary by the sea in
the sixth century of their woe. In their life with
nature, too, a new aspect sympathetic with childhood
emerges; and lastly, though lost, they still live in a
world of their own, as children do. This beautiful
tradition of the Irish race must become a part of the
child-literature of our language.

The Christian element in this last story prepares the
way for the poet's more voluminous and distinctly
religious work — and it is with poets of religion that
he is to be classed — in which he selects his themes

from the saintly legends of the Church, and shows the abundance and power of that life, idealized in holy tradition, which converted the nations and revivified the world. The Reformation was a source of great mortality in literature; and the loss which Protestantism sustained in surrendering the Catholic centuries, with their long record of this ideal life among mankind, was a spiritual deprivation to the northern imagination, which the noble lives of three later centuries have not yet made good. So complete is the gap now, that the times of which these poems reflect the imaginative beauty have the remoteness of a golden age, and in reading the verse a sense of dreaminess invades the mind. This portion of the poet's work makes its mass; and its interest, though various, is so even that one could as easily divide the summer landscape as choose and pick amid its beauty. The subjects are, in the main, from Irish, English, or Roman traditions of the early Church. The tales of St. Patrick, which illustrate the conversion of Ireland, are roughened by the old Bardic strength overcome by the new gospel, and masculine vigour is thus infused into it, while a poetic continuity with the primitive lays is preserved. "Aengus," which is here selected, is a representative instance of these legends, but milder than the most. The tales of Saxon times, which illustrate the conversion of England, are almost pastoral in tone; and again, "St. Cuthbert's Pentecost," here given, is, like "Aengus," only a solitary example. Others of this series are sown with fine

imaginative effects, like that of the lonely Julian
Tower casting the shadow of Rome on the consecra-
tion of Westminster Abbey : —

> " On Saxon feasts she fixed a cold gray gaze;
> 'Mid Christian hymns heard but the old acclaim —
> ' Consul Romanus '; "

or, with eloquent lines, like those on the Primates of
Canterbury : —

> " From their fronts,
> Stubborned with marble from St. Peter's Rock,
> The sunrise of far centuries forth shall flame; "

or, with passages of brief pathos, like Bede's words : —

> " Poor youth ! that love which walks in narrow ways
> Is tragic love, be sure."

The poem, devoted to Cædmon, is especially rich in
such felicities both of image and phrase.

So these Christian poems succeed one another, as
the poet's memory wanders back to the legends of
the Empire on the first establishment of the faith in
Roman lands and along Asian shores, or moves
through mediæval times with Joan of Arc and epi-
sodes of the Cid that recall Cuchullain in their
light-hearted performance of natural deeds, now under
the Cross. The beauty of these separate stories is
equable and full of a softened charm ; but in them,
too, as in the Bardic myths, there abides that distance
of time, which makes them remote, as if they were not
of our own. They are highly pictorial ; and in read-
ing them, each secluded in that silent, old-world air

that encompasses it, one feels that here is a modern
poet, like those early painters of pious heart who spent
their lives in picturing scenes from the life of Christ;
and one recalls, perhaps, some Convent of San Marco
where each monastic cell bears on its quiet walls such
scenes from the shining hand of the Florentine on
whose face fell heaven's mildest light. These poems
of Aubrey de Vere — to characterize them largely —
are scenes from the life of Christ in Man; and there
is something in them — in their gladness, their lumi-
nousness, their peace — which suggests Fra Angelico,
the halo of Christian art.

Yet one reads to little purpose, if he does not dis-
cern also an intellectual element, constant in the poet's
work, which gives it mental as well as spiritual charac-
ter. It is not so much thought, as comprehension,
which his poetry most evinces: that comprehension
which is the genius of the historian and grasps the
governing principles, follows the essential ideas,
watches the doubtful issues of the inward world of
conviction and illusion, of which alone the fate is sig-
nificant. This philosophic interest in history is most
directly expressed in his two dramas, "Alexander
the Great" and "St. Thomas of Canterbury," where
social movements, so irresistible as to be rightly
called providential principles, were centred in great
personalities. In these, his eye sees, not the men
merely, but ideas greater than they, of which, indeed,
they were servants; and this is true, also, of such
single portraits as "Odin," "Constantine," and

"Hildebrand." His prefaces disclose a similar distinctly historical aim in his tales, but their character as particular narratives renders it less obvious; the poetical element in them absorbs and conceals the didactic purpose. He has also occasionally inwoven in his verse more abstract and purely logical argument, of which "The Death of Copernicus" is an example. His sonnets and odes show, in addition, occupation with political and other modern questions. In his single contemporary Irish tale, "The Sisters"—a tale which makes one regret so complete an absorption of his narrative power in other lines—the criticism upon Ireland's history has both edge and weight, and its conversational temper is charming. Together with the gaunt reality of "The Year of Sorrow," this story of the actual reveals the heart of a patriot, near to his living land. Indeed, in whatever division of his verse he approaches the subject of Ireland, his style gathers fire, and often, as must be the case, deepens into melancholy passion. This is shown most characteristically in the ideal conception of Ireland, which he sometimes suggests, as a Sacrificial Nation, whose lot is to show forth spiritual virtues under perpetual earthly misfortune, and it is natural to such a mind; but there is difficulty even in its poetical acceptance, so heavy is the weight of a nation's burden. It is a great conception, but it is not a political idea. It is the young Richard's refuge—"that sweet way I was in to despair." But throughout the entire range of national and religious themes which in a long life-time

the poet has touched, one recognizes a conscientious
and keen thoughtfulness as well as the other qualities
of warmth, imagination, and delight in natural and
moral beauty which are more upon the surface of the
verse ; and to miss this reflective temperament would
be to lose sight of much of the inward significance
of these longer poems.

Of shorter pieces he has written few in comparison
with the body of his work. For one who belongs to the
generation of Tennyson and was the youthful friend of
Wordsworth, the impersonality of his verse is marked.
He paid the tribute to Love, which is required of the
gentle heart, in a few musical lyrics, usually with the
sad cadence ; he paid also his tribute to human liberty
and the general hope of man in some fervid sonnets
that spoke from the breast ; and, lastly, he paid his
tribute to his friends — for he was rich in friendships
— laying his loyal laurel upon each remembered
grave. Finally — to compress much miscellaneous
verse into small space — in " Antar and Zara " he
treated a difficult theme of love with a delicacy and
truth of feeling and a melodic power that justified its
inscription to Tennyson ; in many odes and sonnets
he exhibited the love of nature, the sentiment for land-
scape and its living creatures, and the sense of the
moral power of the external world, which became
a true disciple of Wordsworth and continuer of his
tradition ; and in " The Search after Proserpine," and
elsewhere, he is a neighbour to Shelley. In all this
portion of his work, which is more nearly related to

his own century, except at rare moments he remains impersonal, and deals with ideas through images, in accordance with the great tradition of poetry from the first, for their own and not for the poet's sake.

Such, in general, is the poet's work. But it possesses some qualities which so highly distinguish it in modern verse and give it peculiar character beyond what has been indicated, that a word more must be said. One constant element is its praise of the life of the lowly, in the old Christian sense, as the soil of many virtues, and those the noblest and most endearing. The affinities of his subject-matter, both on the national and the religious side, make this natural; but its source is rather in a true sympathy with lowly lives and knowledge of them, whether among the poor by fate or those who have renounced by choice the things of fortune ; and the ground of this praise — and this is the significant matter — is one that was old when Rousseau was born. So Truth comes into her own again. A second distinguishing element in the verse, as a whole, is its praise of devotion, that loyal surrender to a man or a cause which is one of the ideal passions of Love, and the vital triumph of the soul. To realize what is denoted by this characteristic, and how sharply it severs old and new, it needs only a thought of the quite different way in which — to take the main instance — Tennyson presents this virtue, in his greatest poem of man's life — how maimed and impotent in Arthur, Guinevere, and Lancelot, how doomed to tragic failure in the lesser persons, for Galahad's career is magical, not human ; and the fact that this enfeebling of the principle of devotion is not a trait that, in Tennyson, most strikes a modern reader, measures the distance between the moral ideals that are and those that were. In this, also, Aubrey de Vere returns to the ancient fountains. A third such element in the verse is its purity, which is due, in part, to the fact that the poet is fond of youth, and fills his poems with many fair figures, fresh and ardent and beautiful, and touches with especial delicacy the tenderness of childhood and the grace of boyhood, so that there is a morning air in his world ; but something is also due to his own limpid sincerity and the clarifying power of that spirit which can but represent virtue, however suffering, as joyful. His heroes are always glad. And lastly, to bring these remarks to an end, faith is an element in this verse, not to be passed over in silence. It is faith of the sort not to be rivalled among our poets by any other than Shelley, — faith in the power of truth to subdue mankind to goodness. What to Shelley was dream and vision is here that golden age of the triumph of Christ over the heathen world, when whole nations heard and were baptized. That this is not fanciful paradox a single passage will show, and it affords a striking and useful literary parallel : —

> "They slept not, on the loud-resounding shore
> In glory roaming. Many a feud that night
> Perished; and vengeful vows, now mockery made,
> Lay quenched in their own shame. Far shone the fires

Crowning dark hills with gladness; soared the song;
And heralds sped from coast to coast to tell
How He the Lord of all, no Power Unknown,
But like a man rejoicing in his house,
Ruled the glad earth. . . .

                With earliest red of dawn
Northward once more the winged war-ships rushed,
Swift as of old to that long hated shore —
Not now with axe and torch. His Name they bare
Who linked in one the nations."

This is the feast, the chant, the flame of "Laon and Cythna." In this faith, again, there is the fundamental Christian quality, that older spirit, of which the other elements that have just been mentioned are also branches. Thus, in all this poetry, however its phases be successively turned to the eye, or itself be inwardly searched, there is one light and one breath — the light of the Spirit and the breath thereof. It cannot but have a peculiar, though in its own century almost an exotic, charm. Joy and peace, the first Christian message, spread abroad with its music ; and, heard or unheard, the song of the poet speeds that old evangel.

# NOTE

Of the poems comprised in the following selections, "Cuchullain" is from "The Foray of Queen Meave," and "Naisi's Wooing" from "The Sons of Usnach"; "Oiseen and St. Patrick," "An Old Poet's Love," and "Zara to Antar" are from the several groups of poems similarly entitled; in all other cases, with the exception of the stanza, 'A Farewell,' the poems are given entire. A few titles have been inserted by the editor where none was given by the author. The text of "Cuchullain" follows the earlier edition.

G. E. W.

Beverly, Mass.,
*September*, 1894.

# CONTENTS

# OLD IRISH LAYS

Soul of the Bard! stand up, like thy harp's majestical
    pillar!
  Heart of the Bard, like its arch in reverence bow thee
    and bend!
Mind of the Bard, like its strings be manifold, changeful,
    responsive:
  This is the harp God smites, the harp, man's master
    and friend!

# CUCHULLAIN

THE FORAY OF QUEEN MEAVE *relates the story of the inva-*
*sion of* ULADH *by that Queen, while a spell of enchantment held*
*its people impotent.* CUCHULLAIN *alone arrested her advance;*
*but, on his retirement, her host ravaged the land. On their*
*retreat, the spell being broken, the host of* ULADH *attacked them,*
*and suffered defeat, which* CUCHULLAIN *turned into victory.*
FERGUS *is an exiled chief of* ULADH, *fighting on the side of*
*the invaders. The following passages contain the* DEEDS OF
CUCHULLAIN.

## I

MEANTIME within Murthemné's land its lord,
Cuchullain, musing like a listening hound,
For many a rumour filled that time the air,
Sat in remote Dûn Dalgan all alone,
Chief city of his realm.   On Uladh's verge,
Southward, that lesser realm dependent lay,
Girt by a racing river.   Silent long
He watched : at last he heard a sound like wind
In woods remote ; and earthward bowed his head ;
And said, "That sound is distant thirty leagues,
And huge that host" ; then bade prepare his car,
And southward sped, counsel to hold as wont
With Faythleen nigh to Tara.
      Eve grew dim,
When, lo ! a chariot from the woods emerged
In swift pursuit ; an old man urged the steeds,
A grey old man that chattered evermore,

With blinking eyes that ceased not from amaze,
Now to himself, now to his charioteer.
That sight displeased Cuchullain ; ne'ertheless
He stayed his course ; and Saltain soon drew nigh,
Clamouring, " O son — and when was son like thee —
Forsake not thou thy father !  In old time,
Then when some God had laid on me his hand,
Dectara, my wife, immured me in my house,
Year after year, and weighed the lessening dole ;
But thou, to manhood grown, though even to her
Reverent, didst pluck her from that place usurped,
Lifting thy poor old father."   At that word
Cuchullain left his car, and kissed his sire,
And soothed his wandering wits with meat and wine ;
And spake dissembling : " Lo, these mantles warm !
For thee it was I stored them !  Night is near ;
Lie down and rest."   Thus speaking, with both hands
He spread them deftly forth, and Saltain slept.
Then, tethering first the horses of his sire,
Lastly his own, upon the chill, wet grass
He likewise lay, and slept not.

On, at dawn,

They drave ; but Faythleen, witch perverse of will
That oft through spleenful change her purpose slew,
Had broken tryst ; and northward they returned.
That day Cuchullain clomb a tree-girt rock
And kenned beyond the forest's roof a host
Innumerable, the standards of Queen Meave,
And Fergus, and the great confederate kings.
The warrior eyed them long with bitter smile ;

He spake few words : "At fifty thousand men
I count them." To his father then he turned :
"Haste to Emania ! Bid the Red Branch Knights
Attend me in Murthemné. I till then
Hang on the invaders' flank, a fiery scourge."
  Saltain made answer : "Be it ! northward I ;
But Dectara, thy mother and my wife,
I will not see till thou art by my side ;
For dreadful are her eyes as death or fate ;
And many deem her mad."
                            He spake, and drave
Northward ; nor ceased from chatterings all day long,
Since, like a poplar, vocal was the man
Not less than visible. Meantime his son
Took counsel in his heart, and made resolve
To skirt in homeward course that eastern sea,
The wood primeval 'twixt him and the foe,
Still sallying night and day through alley and glade
And taming thus their pride.
                            Three days went by.
Then stood Cuchullain where great wood-ways met ;
And, lo ! betwixt four yews a warrior's grave,
The pillar-stone above it ! O'er that stone
In mirthful mood he twined an osier wreath,
Cyphering thereon his name in Ogham signs ;
For thus he said : "On no man unawares
Fall I, but warned." The hostile host approached,
And halting stood in wonder at that wreath ;
Yet none could spell the Ogham. Last drew nigh
Fergus, and read it ; on him fell that hour

Memories full dear, and loud he sang and long ;
He sang a warrior's praise, yet named him not ;
He sang : " From name of man to name of beast
A warrior changed ; then mightiest grew of men ! "
And, as he sang, the cheek of Meave grew red.

   Next morn Neara's sons outsped the rest,
Car-borne with brandished spears, and, ere the dew
Was lifted, came to where Cuchullain sat
Beneath an oak, sporting with black-birds twain
That followed him for aye.   Toward the youths
He waved his hand : " Away, for ye are young ! "
In answer forth they flung their spears ; he  caught
      them,
And snapt them on his knee ; next, swift as fire,
Sprang on the twain, and slew them with his sword,
One blow ; anon he loosed their horses' bits,
And they, with madness winged, rejoined the host,
Bearing those headless bulks.   Forth  looked  the
      queen ;
Beheld ; and, trembling, cried : " It might have been
Orloff, my son ! "
                    That eve, at banquet ranged
The warriors questioned Fergus : " Who is best
Among the Uladh chiefs ? "   Ere answer came
King Conor's son self-exiled, Conlinglas,
Upleaping cried, " Cuchullain is his name !
Cuchullain !   From his childhood man was he !
On Eman Macha ever was his thought,
Its walls, its bulwarks, and its Red Branch Knights,
The wonder of the world."   Then told the prince

How, when his mother mocked his zeal, that child
Fared forth alone, with wooden sword and shield,
And fife, and silver ball ; and how he hurled
His little spears before him as he ran,
And caught them ere they fell ; and how, arrived,
He spurned great Eman's gates, and scaled its wall,
And lighted in the pleasaunce of the king,
His mother's brother, Conor Conchobar ;
And how the noble youths of all that land,
There trained in warlike arts, had on him dashed
With insult and with blows ; and how the child
This way and that had hurled them, while the king
Who sat that hour with Fergus, playing chess,
Gazed from his turret wondering.

                      Next he told
How to that child, Setanta first, there fell
Cuchullain's nobler name. "To Eman near
There dwelt an armourer, Cullain was his name,
That earliest rose, and latest with his forge
Reddened the night ; mail-clad in might of his
The Red Branch Knights forth rode ; the bard, the
    chief,
Claimed him for friend. One day, when Conor's self
Partook his feast, the armourer held discourse :
' The Gods have made my house a house of fame ;
The craftsmen grin and grudge because I prosper ;
The forest bandits hunger for my goods,
Yea, and would eat mine anvil if they might —
Trow ye what saves me, Sirs? A Hound is mine ;
Each eve I loose him ; lion-like is he ;

The blood of many a rogue is on his mouth ;
The bravest, if they hear him bay far off,
Flee like a deer ! '    Setanta's shout rang loud
That moment at the gate, and, with it blent,
The baying of that hound !   ' The boy is dead,'
King Conor cried in horror.    Forth they rushed —
There stood he, bright and calm, his rigid hands
Clasping the dead hound's throat !    They wept for
     joy ;
The armourer wept for grief.    ' My friend is dead !
My friend that kept my house and me at peace :
My friend that loved his lord ! '    Setanta heard,
Then first, that cry forth issuing from the heart
Of him whose labour wins his children's bread —
That cry he honours yet.    Red-cheeked he spake :
' Cullain ! unwittingly I did thee wrong !
I make amends.    I, child of kings, henceforth
Abide, thy watch-hound, warder of thy house.'
Thenceforth the ' Hound of Cullain ' was his name,
And Cullain's house well warded."
                         Stern of brow,
The queen arose : " Enough of fables, lords !
Drink to the victory !    Ere yon moon is dead,
We knock at gates of Eman."    High she held
The crimson goblet.    Instant, felt ere heard,
Vibration strange troubled the moonlit air ;
A long-drawn hiss o'er-ran it ; then a cry,
Death-cry of warrior wounded to the death.
They rose ; they gazed around ; Cuchullain stood,
High on a rock.    The swift one said in heart,

"I will not slay her; yet her pride shall die!"
Again that hiss; instant the golden crown
Fell from her head! In wrath she glared around;
Once more that hiss long-drawn, and in her hand
The goblet, shivered, stood! She cast it down;
She cried, "Since first I sat, a queen new-crowned,
Never such ignominy, or spleen of scorn,
Hath mocked my greatness!" Fiercely rushed the
    chiefs
Against the aggressor. Through the high-roofed
    woods
They saw him distant, like a falling star
Kindling the air with speed. Ere long, close by
He stood with sling high holden. At its sound
Ever some great one died! .
               The morrow morn
Cuchullain reached a lawn; tall autumn grass
Whitened within it, but the beech trees round
Were russet brown, the thorn-brakes berry-flushed;
Passing, he raised his spear and launched it forth
Earthward; there stood it buried in the soil
Halfway, and quivering. Loud Cuchullain laughed,
And cried, "It quivers like the tail of swine
Gladdened by acorn feast!" then drew he rein .
And with one sword-stroke felled a youngling birch
And bound it to that spear, and on its bark,
Silvery and smooth, graved with his lance's point
In Ogham characters the words: "Beware!
Unless thou know'st what hand this Ogham traced,
Twine yonder berries 'mid thy young bride's locks,

But spare to tempt that hand!"   An hour passed by,
And Meave had reached the spot.   Chief following
    chief
Drew near in turn; yet none could drag from earth
That spear deep-buried.   Fergus laughed: "Let be,
Connacians!   Task is here for Uladh's hand!"
Then, standing in his car, he clutched the spear
And tugged it thrice.   The third time 'neath his feet
Down crashed the strong-built chariot to the ground.
He laughed!   The queen in anger cried: "March
    on!"
The host advanced, disordered.   Foremost drave
Orloff, Meave's son.   That morning he had wed
A maid, the loveliest in his mother's court,
And yearned to prove his valour in her eyes.
Sudden he came to where Cuchullain stood,
Pasturing his steeds with grass and flower forth held
In wooing, dallying hand.   Cuchullain said,
"The queen's son this!   I will not harm the youth,"
And waved him to depart.   That stripling turned,
Yet, turning, hurled his javelin.   As it flew
Cuchullain caught it, poised it, hurled it home;
It pierced that youth from back to breast; he fell,
Dead on the chariot's floor.   The steeds rushed on,
Wind-swift; and reached the camp.   There sat the
    queen
Throned in her car, listening the host's applause;
In swoon she fell, and lay as lie the dead.
   Next morn again the invaders marched, nor knew
What foe was he who, mocking, thinned their ranks,

Trampled their pride ; who, lacking spear and car,
Viewless by day, by night a fleeting fire,
Dragged down their mightiest, in the death-cry shrill
Drowning the revel. Fergus knew the man,
Fergus alone ; nor yet divulged his name,
Oft muttering : "These be men who fight for Bulls —
I war to shake a Perjurer from his throne,
And count no brave man foe." Again at feast
Ailill made question of the Red Branch Knights.
Fergus replied : "Cuchullain is their best ;
I taught him arms ! Hear of his Knighting Day !
Northward of Eman lies a pleasaunce green.
The Arch-Druid, Cathbad, gazer on the stars,
While there the youths contended, beckoned one
And whispered : ' Happy shall that stripling prove
Knighted this day ! Glorious his life, though brief ! '
That hour Cuchullain stood beyond the wall
South of the city, yet he heard that whisper !
He heard, and cried : ' Enough one day of life,
If great my deeds, and helpful ! ' Swift of foot
He sped to Conor. ' I demand, great king,
Knighthood this day, and knighthood at thy hand.'
But Conor laughed : ' Not fifteen years are thine !
Withhold thyself yet three.' That self-same hour
Old Cathbad entered, and his Druid clan,
And spake : ' King Conor ! by my bed last night
Great Macha stood, the worship of our race,
Our strength in realms unseen. "Arise," she said ;
"To Conor speed ; to him report my will ;
That youth knighted this day is mine Elect !

I, Macha, send him forth!"

                              "'She spake and passed ;
Trembled the place like cliffs o'er ocean caves ;
Like thunder underground I heard her wheels
In echoes slowly dying.'

                      " Fixed and firm
King Conor stood.   Sternly he made reply :
' Queen Macha had her day and ruled ; far down
Doubtless this hour she rules, or rules aloft ;
I rule in Eman and this Uladh realm ;
I will not knight a stripling ! '   Prophet-like
Up-towered old Cathbad, and his sons black-stoled.
This way and that they rolled prophetic bolts
Three hours, and brake with warnings from the stars
And mandates from the synod of the Gods
The king's resolve.   At last he cried, ' So be it !
Since Gods, like men, grow witless, be it so !
The worse for Eman, and great Macha's land !
Stand forth, my sister's son ! '   He spake and bound
The Geisa, and the edicts, and the vows
Of that dread Red Branch Order on the boy,
And gave him sword and lance.

                        " An eye star-keen
That boy upon them fixed, and, each on each,
Smote them.   They snapt in twain.   Laughing, he
     cried :
' Good art thou, Uncle mine, but these are base ;
I need a warrior's weapons ! '   Conor signed ;
Then brought his knaves ten swords, and lances ten ;
Cuchullain eyed them each and snapt them all,

The concourse marvelling. 'Varlets,' cried the king,
'Bring forth my arms of battle !' These in turn
Cuchullain proved ; they brake not. Up they dragged
A battle-car. Cuchullain leaped therein ;
With feet far set he spurned its brazen floor
That roared and sank in fragments. Chariots twelve
Successive thus he vanquished. 'Uncle mine,
Good art thou,' cried the youth ; 'but these are base !'
King Conor signed, 'My car of battle !' Leagh,
The charioteer, forth brought it with the steeds ;
Cuchullain proved that war-car and it stood.
Careless he spake : 'So, well ! The car will serve !
Abide ye my return.'

                 " He shook the reins ;
He called the horses by their names well-known ;
He dashed through Eman's gateway as a storm.
Far off a darksome wood and darksome tower
Frowned over Mallok's wave ; therein abode
Three bandit chieftains, foes to man ; well pleased
Those bandits eyed the on-rushing car and youth,
Exulting in their prey. That youth, arrived,
Summoned those three to judgment ; forth they
    thronged,
They and their clan ; he slew them with his sling,
The three ; and severed with his sword their heads,
And fixed them on the chariot's front. His mood
Changed then to mirthful ; fleeter than the wind
Six stags went by him, stateliest of the herd ;
Afoot he chased them, caught them, bound them fast
Behind the chariot rail. Birds saw he next,

White as a foam-wreath of their native sea,
Spotting the glebe new turned.   A net lay near ;
He caged them ; next he tied them to his car,
Wide-winged, and wailing loud.   To Eman's towers
Returned he last with laughter ; at its gate
The king, the chiefs, grey Druids, maids red-cloaked,
Agape to see him ; on his chariot's front
The grim heads of those bandits ; in its rear
Those stags wide-horned ; and, high o'erhead, the
        birds ! "

    The laughter ceased ; then spake King Conor's son :
"Recount the wonder of those fairy steeds
That drag Cuchullain's war-car ! "   Fergus then,
Despite Queen Meave, who plaited still her robe
With angry hectic hand, the tale began.

    "Cuchullain paced the herbage thin that clothes
Slieve Fuad's summit.   On that airy height
A wan lake glittered, whitening in the blast,
Pale plains around it.   From beneath that lake
Emerged a horse foam-white !   Cuchullain saw,
And straightway round that creature's neck high
        held
Locked the lithe arms no struggles could unwind.
That courser, baffled, clothed his strength with speed ;
From cliff to cliff he sped ; cleared at a bound
Inlet and rocky rift ; nor stayed his course,
Men say, till he had circled Erin's Isle ;
Panting then lay he, on his conqueror's knee
Resting his head ; thenceforth that conqueror's friend,
His ' Liath Macha.'   Gentle-souled is she —

'Sangland,' the wild one's comrade. As the night
Sank on those huge red-berried woods of yew,
Lough Darvra's girdle, from the ebon wave
She issued, darker still. Softly she paced,
As though with woman's foot, the grassy marge
In violets diapered, and laid her head
Upon Cuchullain's shoulder. In his wars
Emulous those mated marvels drag his car ;
In peace he yokes them never."

                        Fergus rose :
"Night wanes," he said, "and tasks await my hand."
Passing the throne he whispered thus the queen :
"The Hound of Uladh is your visitant
Both day and night." The cheek of Meave grew
    pale.


## II

THUS ever day by day, and night by night,
Through strength of him that 'mid the royal host
Passed, and re-passed like thought, the bravest fell ;
For ne'er against the inglorious or the small
Cuchullain raised his hand. Then Ailill spake :
" Let Fergus seek that champion in the woods,
Gift-laden, and withdraw him from his king."
But Fergus answered : " Sue and be refused !
That great one loves his country. Heard ye never
How when King Conor's sin, that forfeit pledge
Plighted with Usnach's sons, had left the Accursèd
Crownless, and Eman's bulwarks in the dust,

Her elders on Cuchullain worked, what time
He came my work of vengeance to complete?
They said : ' Cuchullain loves his land o'er all !
The man besides, though terrible to foes,
Is tender to the weak.   Through Eman's streets
Send ye proclaim, " Will any holy maid
To save the city take her station sole
On yonder bridge, at parting of the ways,
That city's Emblem-Victim, robed in black
Down from her girdle to the naked feet ;
Above that girdle this alone — the chains
Of Eman's gate, circling that virgin throat
And down at each side streaming?   It may be
That dread one will relent, pitying in her
Great Uladh's self despoiled of robe and crown,
Her raiment bonds and shame." '   Of Eman's maids
But one, the best and purest, gave consent.
Alone she stood at parting of the ways ;
While near and nearer yet that war-car drew,
Wide-eyed she stood, death-pale ; it stopped ; she
        spake :
' Eman, thy Mother, stands a widow now,
Despoiled of crown, her raiment bonds and shame ;
And many a famished babe that wrought no ill
Lies 'mid her ruins wailing.'   To the left
The warrior turned his steeds.   The land was saved."
   Then spake the kings confederate : " Hard albeit
That task, to draw Cuchullain from his charge,
Seek him, and proffer terms !"   Fergus next morn
Made way through those sea-skirting woods, and cried

Three times, "Setanta;" and Cuchullain heard,
And knew that voice, and, beaming, issued forth,
And clasped his ancient master round the neck,
And led him to his sylvan cell.    Therein
Long time they held discourse of ancient days,
Heaven-fair through mist of years.    The youthful host
Set forth their rural feast, whate'er the woods
And they that in them dwelt, swine-herds and hinds,
Yielded, their best : nor lacked it minstrel strain,
Bird-song  by  autumn  chilled,  that  brake  through
        boughs
Lit by unwarming sunshine.    Banquet o'er,
Fergus disclosed the terms of Meave, and gifts
By her and Ailill sent.    Cuchullain rose
And curtly answered : "Never will I break
My vow ; nor wrong the land ; nor sell my king."
Fergus too royal was to hear surprised,
Or grieved, his friend's resolve, nor touched again
Upon that pact unworthy.    Happier themes
Succeeded, mirthful some.    Of these the last
Made sport of Ailill.    Fergus spake : "One night
I sped to Meave's pavilion swift of foot ;
War-tidings wait not.    Ailill from afar
Furtively followed, stung by jealous spleen.
The queen had passed into the inner tent ;
I sought her there.    In the outer Ailill marked
My sword, that morning thither sent, a loan,
For Meave had vowed to out-brave its hilt with gems
Blazoning her zone.    His wrath was changed to joy !
He snatched it up ; he cried, ' Hail, forfeit mine !

c

Hail *Eric* just !' and laughed his childish laugh.
Since then he neither frowns on me nor smiles.
He will not let me rule his foolish kings ;
Yet, deeming still my sword a charm 'gainst fate,
Wears it.   An apter one I keep for him ;
One day 'twill raise a laugh !"   In graver mood
At parting Fergus spake : " I grant that pact
Proposed by Meave fitter for her than thee ;
Yet hide not if thou know'st of terms more meet."
To whom Cuchullain : " Fergus, terms there be,
Other and meeter.   I divulge them not ;
Divine them he that seeks them !"   On the morn
Fergus declared his tidings to the chiefs
In synod met.   A recreant churl arose,
And thus gave counsel : " Lure Cuchullain here
On pretext fair ; and slay him at the feast."
Against that recreant Fergus hurled his spear,
And slew him, and continued : " Hundreds six,
Our best, have perished, and our march is slow.
Now, warriors, hear my counsel, and my terms ;
Cuchullain scorns your gifts — of such no more !
'Twixt southern Erin and my Uladh's realm
Runs Neeth ; across that river lies a ford ;
Speak to Cuchullain : ' By that ford stand thou,
Guarding thy land.   Against thee, day by day,
Be ours to send one champion — one alone.
While lasts that strife, forbear the host beside ! ' "

Then roared the kings a long and loud applause,
Since wise appeared that counsel ; faith they pledged,
And sureties in the hearing of the Gods :

Likewise Cuchullain, when his friend returned,
Made answer : " Well you guessed ! a month or more
My strength will hold ; meantime, our Uladh arms."
To seal that pact he sought the hostile camp,
And shared the banquet. Wondering, all men gazed ;
And maidens, lifted on the warriors' shields,
Gladdened, so bright that youthful face. At morn
Meave, when the chief departed, kissed his cheek :
" Pity," she said, " that such a one should die ! "
The one sole time that Meave compassion felt.

That eve Cuchullain drank the wave of Neeth,
And wading reached Murthemné's soil, his charge,
And knelt, and kissed it. As the sun declined,
He clomb a rocky height, and northward gazed,
And cried : " Ye Red Branch warriors, haste ! I keep
The ford ; but who shall guard it when I die?"

Next morning by that stream the fight began,
Two champions face to face ; and, every morn,
Rang out, renewed, that combat ; every eve
Again went up from that confederate host
The shout of rage. Daily their bravest died,
Thirty in thirty days. Feerbraoth fell,
And Natherandal, though the Druid horde
Above his javelins, carved at set of moon
From the ever-sacred holly stem, had breathed
Vain consecration, and with futile salve
Anointed them ; confuted soon they sailed
In ignominy adown that seaward tide
With him that hurled them. Eterconnel next,
Dalot, and Cuir : — yet he who laid them low

Was beardless at the lip.   While thus they strove,
A second month went by.

        Such things beholding,
The queen was moved ; and in her grew one day
Craving for Cruachan.   But on her ear
Rolled forth that hour the lowings of that Bull,
Cualgné's Donn ; for he from Daré's house
Had heard, though far, the clamours of the host,
And answered rage with rage.   Then Meave resolved,
" Though all my host should perish to a man,
This foot shall tread no more my native plains
Save with that Bull in charge ! "

          To her by night
Came Cailitin, who ever walked by night
Shunning mankind, and Fergus most of all, —
Cailitin, father of the Magic Clan,
And thus addressed her : " Place in me thy trust ;
I hate Cuchullain, for he scorns my spells,
Resting his hope on virtue.   In thy camp
Ferdia bides, a Firbolg feared of all.
Win him to meet Cuchullain.   They in youth
Were friends ; to slay that friend will lay a hand
Icy as death upon Cuchullain's heart.
Ferdia dies — thus much mine art foreshews ;
Then I, since magic spells have puissance most
Not on the body sick but spirit depressed,
Fall on him with my seven and twenty sons,
Magicians all.   One are we ; thence with one
May fight, thy pledge unflawed.   A drop of blood
Shed by our swords, though small as beetle's eye,

Costs him his life." Fiercely the queen replied,
"A Firbolg! Never!" Cailitin resumed:
"Then send for Lok Mac Favesh!"

                                 With the morn
Mac Favesh sought her tent. Direful his mien;
Massive his stride; his body brawny and huge;
For, though of Gaelic race, the stock of Ir,
With him was mingled giant blood of old,
Wild blood of Nemedh's brood, that hurled sea rocks
'Gainst the Fomorian. Oft the advancing tide
Drowned both, in battle knit. Before the queen
Boastful the sea-king laid his club, and spake:
"Queen, though to combat with a beardless boy
Affronts my name, my lineage, and my strength,
His petulance shall vex thine eye no more!
Uladh is thine to-morrow!" At the dawn,
By hundreds girt, the great ones of his clan,
Down drave he to the ford, and onward strode
Trampling the last year's branches strewn hard by
That snapped beneath him. Hides of oxen seven
Sustained the brazen bosses of his shield;
And forth he stretched a hand that might have grasped
A tiger's throat and choked him. O'er his helm
Hovered an imaged demon raven-black.
Cuchullain met him; hours endured the strife,
That mountained strength triumphant now, anon
Cuchullain's might divine. Then first that might
Was fully tasked. Upon the bank that day
Stood up a Portent seen by none save him,
A Shape not human. Terribly it fixed

On him alone its never-wandering eye ;
The dread Mor Reega, she that from the skies
O'er rules the battle-fields, and sways at will,
This way or that, the sable tides of death.
He gazed ; and, though incapable of fear,
Awe, such as heroes feel, possessed his heart ;
Its beatings shook his brain ; his corporal mould
Throbbed as a branch against some river swift ;
And backward turned his hair like berried trails
Of thorn athwart the hedge.   Three several times
He saw her, yet fought on.   With beckoning hand
At last that Portent summoned from the main
A huge sea-snake ; round him it twined its knots ;
Then on Cuchullain fell the rage from heaven ;
A sword-blow, and that vast sea-worm lay dead !
A sword uplifted, and Mac Favesh fell
Prone on the shuddering flood.   In death he cried :
" Lay me with forehead turned to Uladh's realm ; —
They shall not say that fugitive I died."
Cuchullain wrought his will ; then, bleeding fast,
Stood upright, leaning on his spear aslant ;
A warrior battle-wearied.
                                        From the bank
Meantime, the dark magician, Cailitin,
He and his sons, with wide and greedy eyes,
That still, like one man's eyes, together moved,
Had watched that fight, counting each drop that fell
Down from Cuchullain's wounds.   When faint he
        stood,
At once their cry rang out like one man's cry ;

Like one their seven and twenty javelins flew;
As swift, Cuchullain caught them on his shield;
An instant more, and all that horde accursed
Was dealing with him.   From the trampled ford
Went up a mist of spray that veiled that strife,
Though pierced by demon cries, and flash beside
Of demon swords.   O'er it at last up-towered,
On-borne — such power to blend have spirits impure —
A single Form — as when o'er seas storm-laid
The watery column reels, and draws from heaven
The cloud, and drowns the ship — a single Form,
And Head, and Hand, clutching Cuchullain's crest;
Even then he sank not.   O'er that mist of spray
Glittered his sword.   There fell a silence strange;
That spell, which made the many one, dissolved;
Slowly that mist dispersed; and on the sands
That false Enchanter lay with all his sons,
Black, bleeding bulks of death.

                              Amid them stood
Cuchullain; near him, seen by him alone,
That dread Mor Reega, now benign.   She spake:
" I hated thee, because thy trust was less
In me than Virtue's aid.   I hate no more.
Be strong ! a trial waits thee worse than this —
No man is friend of mine till trial-proved."
   Yet, sad at heart, that eve Cuchullain clomb
His wonted rock, and faint with loss of blood,
And mused: " My strength must lessen day by day;"
And northward gazed, thus murmuring: " All too
      late

To save the land those Red Branch Knights will
    come
When I am dead —
My war-car, and my war-steeds are far off,
And I am here alone." That night through grief
He slept not ; for the Magic Clan had power,
Though dead, to lean above him as a cloud
Darkening his spirit, and to grief and shame
Changing bright days gone by.

                   While thus he sat,
He saw, not distant, on the forest floor,
In moonbeams clad, though moon was near him none,
A pure and princely presence. Lithe his form
In youthful prime ; chain armour round him clung,
Bright as if woven of diamonds. Glad his eye ;
Dulcet his voice as strain from Elfin glen,
Far heard o'er waters. Thus that warrior spake :
" My child, an ancestor of thine am I,
Great Ethland's son, in sacred battle slain,
Fencing my people from an alien foe.
Among the Sidils now, and fairy haunts
Moon-lit, and under depths of lucent lakes,
Gladness I have who in my day had woe,
And youth perpetual though I died in age.
Thou need'st repose ; for sixty days thine eyes
Have closed reluctant. Sleep a three days' sleep,
Whilst I, thy semblance bearing, meet thy foes."
Thus spake the youth, then sang Lethean song
Wedded with virgin song from waters near,
And, straight, Cuchullain slept. Three days gone by,

Again that vision came.  " Arise," he said ;
The warrior rose ; and lo ! his wounds were healed ;
Down sped he to the river.
                                        Waiting there
Stood up Iarion, champion of the queen, —
There stood, nor thence returned.   Eochar next
Perished, then Tubar, Chylair, Alp, and Ord,
In all full ninety warriors.   Ninety days
Had fled successive since that strife began,
When, on the ninetieth eve, at set of sun,
His strength entire, and victory eagle-winged
Fanning his ardent cheek, Cuchullain scaled
Once more that specular rock.   Within his heart
Spirit illusive, that with purpose veiled
Oft tries the loftiest most, this presage sang :
" Southward, not distant, thou shalt see them march
At last, that Red Branch Order, in their van
Thy Conal Carnach !"   Other spectacle
Met him, a chariot small with horses small,
And, o'er the axle bent, a small old man,
Urging them feebly on.   It was his sire !
T'wards him Cuchullain rushed ; the old man wept,
For gladness wept, and afterwards for woe,
Kissing the wounds unnumbered of his son.
Reverent, Cuchullain led him to his cell ;
Reverent, he placed before him wine and meat ;
Nor questioned yet.   The old man satisfied,
Garrulity returned, though less than once,
Now quelled by patriot passion.   Thus he spake :
" Setanta ! son of mine ! I bring ill news.

Uladh is mad ; the Red Branch House is mad ;
Mad as thy mother ; all the world are mad,
And I that was a mad man twenty years
Am now of Uladh's sons most nigh to sane.
Attend my tidings !   Through the realm I sped.
A mist hung o'er it heavy, and on her sons
Imbecile spirit, and a heartless mind,
And base soul-sickness.   Evermore I cried,
' Arise ! the stranger's foot is on your soil ;
They come to stall their horses in your halls ;
To slay your sons ; enslave your spotless maids ;
Alone my son withstands them !'   Shrewd of eye
Men answered, ' Merchant ; see thy wares be sound !
No lack-wits we !'   Old seers I saw that decked
Time-honoured foreheads with a jester's crown.
I saw an ollamb trample under foot
His sacred Oghams ; next I saw him grave
His own blear image on the tide-washed sands,
Boasting, 'The unnumbered ages here shall stoop,
Honouring true Wisdom's image.'   Shepherds set
The wolf to guard their fold.   The wittol bade
The losel lead his wife to feast and dance ;
Young warriors looked on maids with woman's eyes.
I drave to Daré's Dûn ; his loud-voiced sons
Adored the Donn Cualgné as their sire,
And called their sire a calf.   To Iliach's tower
I sped ; he answered, ' What ! the foe ! they come !
Climb we yon apple trees, and garner store !
Wayfarers need much victual !'   Onward next
To Sencha's castle ; on the roof he knelt,

Self-styled the kingdom's chief astrologer,
Waiting the unrisen stars.   To Olchar's Dûn
I journeyed ; wrapped in rags the strong man lay,
Thin from long fast; with eyelids well-nigh closed ;
Not less beneath them lay a gleaming streak :
' Awake me not,' he said : ' a dormouse I !
'Till peace returns I simulate to sleep.'
I sought the brothers Nemeth ; one his eyes
Bent on the smoke-wreath from his chimney's top,
One on the foam-streak wavering down the stream ;
While each a finger raised, and said, 'Tread light !
All earth is grass o'er glass ! '   I sought the mart ;
Men babbled : ' Bid the Druids find the king ! '
I sought the Druids' College ; in a hall,
Reed-strewn to smother sound, they held debate
On Firbolg and Dedannan contracts pledged
Ere landed first the Gael.   The Red Branch House
Was changed to hospital; and knights full-armed
Nodded o'er lepers' beds.   I sought the king ;
From hall deserted on to hall I roamed ;
I found him in his armoury walled around
With mail of warriors dead.   There stood, or lay,
The chiefs by Uladh worshipped.   Nearest, crouched
Great Conal Carnach patting of his sword
Like nurse that lulls an infant.   On his throne
Sat Conchobar in miniver and gold ;
His eyes were on his grandsire's shield that breathed
At times a sigh athwart the steel-lit gloom ;
Around his lips an idiot's smile was curled :
' What will be, will be,' spake the king at last :

' All things go well.' "
                         Thus Saltain told his tale.
One thing he told not — how, a moment's space,
The passion of an old man's scorn had wrought
Deliverance strange for that astonished throng,
High miracle of nature.   He, the man
Despised since youth, the laughter of the crowd,
Himself restored to youth by change like death,
Had rolled his voice abroad, a mighty voice.
They heard it ; from their trance they burst ; they
        stood,
Radiant once more with mind !   They stood till died
The noble anger's latest echo.   Then
That mist storm-riven put forth once more its hand,
And downward dragged its prey.
                             Upon his feet,
When ceased his father's voice, Cuchullain sprang ;
That rage divine which gave him strength divine
Had fallen on him from heaven.   He raised his
        hands,
And roared against the synod of the Gods
That suffer shames below.   Beyond the stream
That host confederate heard and armed in haste,
And slept that night in armour.   Far away
Compassion touched the strong hearts of the Gods,
The strongest most — Mor Reega's.   Ere that cry
Had left its last vibration on the air,
High up the Battle-Goddess, adamant-mailed,
Was drifting over Uladh.   Eman's towers
Flashed back her helmet's beam.   With lifted spear

She smote the brazen centre of her shield
Three times; and thunder, triple-bolted, rolled
Three times from sea to sea.   The spell was snapped.
Humanity returned to man !   The first
Who woke was Leagh, Cuchullain's charioteer ;
Forth from the opprobrious mist he passed, like ship
That cleaves the limit of some low marsh-fog
And sweeps into main ocean.   Forth he rushed,
Forth to Cuchullain's chariot-house, and dragged
Abroad that war-car feared of all — men say
The axle burnt beneath his hand — and yoked
White Liath Macha, and his comrade black,
And dashed adown the vacant, echoing streets,
And passed the gateway towers ; the warders slept ;
Beyond them, propped against the city wall,
A cripple crunched his mouldering crust.   Still on
He rushed, the reins forth shaking and the scourge,
Clamouring and crying : " Haste, Cuchullain's steeds !
On, Liath Macha !   Sable Sangland, on !
Your master needs you !   Ay ! ye know it now !
The blood-red nostril smells the fight far off !
On to Murthemné, and Cualgné's hills,
And Neeth's remembered ford !"   Unseen he drave ;
So, slowly, clinging still to brake and rock,
And oft re-settling, vanished from the land
The insane mist.   That hurricane of wheels
Not less was heard by men who nothing saw ;
On stony plain, in hamlet and in vale.
They muttered, as in sleep, " Deliverance comes."

## III

MEANTIME the queen, ere dawned that ninetieth morn,
Mused, ill at ease : "Daily my people die,
And many a stormy brow on me is bent.
What if they turn on me like starving hounds
That rend their huntsman?"    In her ear once more
Sounded the word of Cailitin : "The man
To fight Cuchullain is the man he loves.
His death were death to both."    Then came the kings
Confederate, saying, "Send Ferdia forth !
Ferdia is the mightiest of our host ;
Ferdia is Cuchullain's chief of friends ;
Westward of Alba in the Isle of Skye,
Scatha, that rock-browed northern warrioress,
In amplest lore of battles trained them both.
Except the Gae-Bulg, every feat of arms
Is known to each alike."
                              The queen gave way.
She sent her herald to the man she scorned
With offers huge, tract vaster than his own,
Not barren like his mountains billow-beat,
But laughing in the lap of Ai's plains ;
A war-car deftly carved and ribbed with brass ;
And, for his clansmen, raiment of all dyes,
Twelve suits.    A stalwart man, yet fair as strong,
The Firbolg towered, dark-eyed, dark-haired, pale-
        faced,
Unlike the Gael.    Melodious was his voice,
But deeper than a lion's.    Ceaseless thought

On immemorial wrongs — he brooded still
O'er glories of Moytura and Tailltenn,
Their great assemblies and their solemn games,
And kingly graves — had stamped upon his brow
Perpetual shade ; and ever, on the march,
If high on crags there stood some Gaelic tomb
Wind-worn a thousand years, he passed it by
With face averse, muttering, " New men ! New men !
We note not such ! " The herald's task discharged,
He answered thus, not turning : " Tell your queen
That I, a Firbolg, serve, but not for hire,
A cause not mine. Cuchullain is my friend.
Better I died than he."

                         O'er-awed though wroth
The queen despatched in statelier embassage
Three warriors, and three ollamhs, and three bards.
With reverence they addressed him. " Chief and
     Prince !
True prince, though scion of a house deject,
The queen, who judges all men by their deeds,
This day hath in thine honour made a feast
And sues to it thy presence. Kings alone
Partake that banquet ; Ailill first, and she
Of princesses the fairest, Finobar ! "
Scornful the Firbolg answered, " Finobar !
She whose bright face hath frosted with death's white
Full four score faces of war-breathing men
Sent to that Ford successive ! Let it be !
Tell them I join their feast ; tell them beside
Their bribe shall prove base gold ! "

                              In mantle blue
Clasped by a silver torque, and silver belt
Enringed with silver rings innumerable,
That evening from his tent Ferdia strode
With large attendance.   Ailill and the queen
Received him on their threshold.   At the board
Princes alone had place.   High up, o'er each,
Glittered upon the wall his blazoned shield.
King Ailill placed Ferdia on his right ;
Beyond him sat the Princess.   In her ear
Her mother whispered as she neared that seat ;
She answered with her eyes.
                              Well-stricken harp
Gladdened that festive throng ;  and Ailill told,
The rage of hunger lessening by degrees,
Full many a tale of the heroic past,
When, youthful yet, he ranged 'mid friends and foes —
Such men as breathed no longer.   Servitors
Brimmed oft the goblets ;  and Ferdia's brow,
As song to song succeeded, tale to tale,
Remitted its first sternness.   Finobar
Unconsciously had dropped her jewelled hand
Not far from his ;  her large and dusky eyes,
Shyly at first from his withdrawn, at last
Full frankly met them ;  on her lips the smile
Increased, though waveringly, then waned, not died,
And in it sadness mingled as she spake :
" But late yon harper told us of a dream —
My earliest of remembered dreams was sad ;
I saw some princess of your earlier stock

Whose lover late had perished, slain in fight
By ours, methought then recent.   At her feet —
Why there I scarcely know — I made lament :
' All thou hast lost for thy sake I renounce ;
For me, like thee, no bridal rites forever !
Dead on thy marriage garland lies mine own.
For, lo ! the stain accursed is on our sword ;
Thy race came first ; this Island should be theirs ! ' "
Ferdia listened ; and the icy pride
Thawed in his bosom.   With a sudden change
The jubilant music into martial soared,
Wild battle-chaunt.   Upon the warrior's hand,
Still nigh to hers, there lay a scar.   With eye
Reverently dewed the princess gazed thereon :
" Yes, of your war-deeds I have heard so long,
It seems as though since childhood — Whence  that
        wound ?
What battle left it there ?   What sister bound it ?
I would that sister were my sister too,
Partaker of my heart, my hope, my life.
I have no youthful friend ! "   She paused ; again
But now with paler cheek, and hurried, spake :
" Beware my mother !   She would send you forth
Her knight to meet Cuchullain !   Shun that man !
Cuchullain spares not ; four score warriors dead
Avouch it.   Chief of Gaels he is !   Ah me !
The last great battle 'twixt the old race and new
Would find the same sad ending as the first."
The Firbolg frowned ; she faltered, " Am I false,
False to my race " — and tears were in her voice —

D

" False to my race, who cannot wish such ending? "
She paused ; again she questioned of his wars;
He told her of his sire's.   Like one who thinks,
Not speaks, she murmured low, " A soothsayer
Thus warned my mother — I was then a child —
' Bring not that maid to war-fields !   She shall die
Grieving for some dead warrior.' "
       Speaking thus,
Though false, the princess lied not.
        Changed once more
The martial songs to amorous and of mirth,
And once again the torches' golden flame
Laughed on the cup new-brimmed.   Again she spake,
That lovesome one : " I love not songs of love !
Better the war-song !   Best, methinks, of all
That lullaby, half war and sorrow half,
Breathed by some bride while o'er her wounded lord
Softly descends the sleep : — so softly sank
Cold dews of evening on this flower still wet."
She took it from her breast, and held it near ;
He smelt it ; kissed it ; kept it.   With a smile
She added, " For your sister?   Have you one?
If so, 'tis likely she resembles me.
They chide me oft : 'No Gaelic face is thine,
Dark-eyed, dark-browed, a rebel since its birth ! ' "
She ceased ; again she spake : " Even now, methinks,
That lullaby I spake of I can hear !
Is it for thee, my friend, or Cuchullain?"
That hand, of flower amerced, drew nearer yet
To his.   That smile had passed.   Tearful she turned

On him those luminaries of love and death,
Her eyes, like stars in midnight waters glassed;
Turned them, but spake no longer.  Through his
    brain
Shivered their shrouded lustre; through his blood.
The sanguine currents from the warrior's heart
Long sad, to female sympathies unused,
Drank up at once that splendour, and the tears
That splendour's strange eclipse.

                    And yet, that hour,
Seen in some lonelier region of his soul,
Another presence, O how different! stood.
Again, that hour, he saw those guileless eyes,
Blue as the seas they gazed on; saw once more
That hair like winter sunshine, brow snow-white,
That unvoluptuous form and virginal,
That love-unwakened breast with love for all,
Those hands that knew not what their touch con-
    ferred,
Those blithesome, wave-washed, scarce divided feet :—
The huge cliff smiled upon her; seemed to say,
"Ah, little nursling mine!  Ah, tender child
Of winds and rocks untender!"

                    Had he loved?
Sadness is celibate and eremite.
His converse long had been with injuries past,
In Scatha's Isle with frowning crags and clouds—
Ay, but with one beside, a friend, his nearest,
Who loved the daughter of that warrioress
And sued Ferdia's help in love.   Ferdia

Had never spoken love ; nor thought, "I love ;"
And yet, that hour, was false.
                       A hundred harps
Rang out together, and the feast was o'er.
Murmured the rose-red lips ; but what they said
He heard not.   Mournfully at last withdrew
That hand so near to his — he had not touched it —
Those eyes, like eyes fated thenceforth to bear
One image on till death.   She joined her mother.
    The queen, as he departed, took his hand.
Alone they stood ; she spake : " That noble scorn,
Which spurned a bribe, approves a Firbolg's worth.
'Twas Ailill sent that herald ; 'twas not I.
I know you now, and proffer royal terms
Confirmed by guarantee of all our kings.
Accept this combat ; and the princess wed !
Ferdia !   I have made that offer thrice
To three dead warriors with the king's consent,
Never, till now, with hers !"
                     He pledged his word.
The battle day was fixed ; the morrow morn.
She took that glittering torque whose splendours
     clasped
Her mantle red ; with it his mantle bound.
Then with attendance to his tent he passed.
    Meantime, that night within his forest lair
In dreams Cuchullain lay, and saw in dreams,
Not recent fights, but ocean and that Isle
Where with Ferdia he had dwelt in youth,
With Scatha — and another.   And in dream

He mused : " The dearest of my friends survives.
These wars will pass ; Ferdia, then, and I,
Thenceforth, are one for aye ! " That self-same hour
The Firbolg slowly woke from troubled sleep,
Murmuring, as one in trance, " Against my friend !
Against my only friend ! " His clansmen watched
With gloomy brows his arming. One sole man
They feared — that man, Cuchullain. Morn the while
Was dawning, though she raised nor glowing cheek
Nor ardent eyes, with silver wand not gold
Striking the unkindling portals of the East ;
And, ere the sun had risen, Ferdia bathed
Three times his forehead in the frosty stream ;
And bade his charioteer attend ; and drave,
Begirt by stateliest equipage of war,
Down to the river's brim. In regal pomp
The host confederate followed, keen to watch,
With Meave, and Ailill, and with Finobar,
All passions of a fight unmatched till then
On warfields of the immemorial world ;
While clustered here and there, on rock or mound,
Minstrel and food-purveyor, groom, and leech,
With healing herbs and charms.

                The sun arose,
And smote the forest roof, dew-saturate,
As onward dashed through woodlands to the Ford
Cuchullain's war-car. Nearer soon it rolled,
Crushing the rocks. Above those wondrous steeds
That Great One glittered through low mist of morn,
Splendour gloom-veiled. Ferdia's charioteer

Half heard, half saw him.   Spirit-rapt, yet awed,
Perforce thus sang he, standing near the marge :
    " I hear the on-rushing of the Car !   I see
There throned that warrior, not of mortal mould,
Swathed in the morning.   Dreadful are his wheels ;
Dreadful as breaker arched, when on its crest
Stands Fear, and Fate upon the rock-strewn shore ;
But not sea-rocks they crush, those brazen wheels,
But realms, and peoples, and the necks of men.
    " I see the War-Car !   Terrible it comes,
Four-peaked ; and o'er those peaks a shadowy pall
Pavilioning dim crypt and caves of death.
I see it by the gleam of spears high held,
The glare of circling Spirits.   Lo ! the same
I saw far northward drifting, months gone by,
Ere yet that madness quelled the northern land."
    Then cried Ferdia, stationed where huge trees
Shut out unwelcome vision : " For a bribe
Thou seest these portents, singing of my death !"
    Once more, in agony prophetic, he :
" The man within that car is Uladh's Hound !
What hound ?   No stag-hound of the storm-swept
        hills ;
No watch-hound watching by a merchant's store.
The hound he is that tracks the steps of doom ;
The hound of realms o'er-run, and hosts that fly ;
The hound that laps the blood ! "
                                    Again he sang :
" The Hound of Uladh is a hound with wings ;
A hound man-headed !   Yea, and o'er that head

Victory and empire, like two eagles paired,
Sail onward, tempest-pinioned.   Endless morn,
Before him fleeting over seas and lands,
With shaft retorted, lights his chariot-beam.
That chariot stays not, turns not ; on it comes,
Like torrent shooting from a tall cliff's brow,
Level long time ; then downward borne !"

                         " A bribe !"

Once more Ferdia cried ; " A bribe ! a lie !
Traitor ! for Ailill's gold and gold of Meave,
Thou sing'st thy master's death-song !"

                         By the stream
Cuchullain stood, nor yet he knew his foe ;
That foe who slowly to the Ford advanced,
Full panoplied, and in his hand a spear.
Long gazed they, each on each.   Cuchullain spake :
" Welcome howe'er thou com'st, Ferdia !   Once
In Scatha's Isle far otherwise thou camest,
Morn after morn, with tidings fresh of war,
Plaything and pastime of our brother brands.
This day thou com'st invader of my land
Murthemné, bulwark broad of Uladh's realm ;
Thou com'st to burn my cities, spoil my flocks —
A change there is, Ferdia !"   Stern of brow,
The Firbolg answered : " Friends we were ; not peers ;
The younger thou.   'Twas thine to yoke my steeds ;
Arm me for fight.   A stripling hopes this day
With brandished spear to make a mountain flee !
Son of the Gael ! long centuries since, thy race
Trampled my race ; their vengeance hour is near ;

I bid thee to depart!"   To him his friend :
" Ferdia, in the old days on Scatha's Isle
Thou wert my tribe, my house, my stock, my race !
Questioned I then on battle-plain, or when
On frosty nights we crouched beneath one rug,
Ancestral claims, traditions of the clan?—
A change there is, Ferdia ! "

      Thus with words
Or mild, or stern, in hope to save not slay,
Those friends contended.   Sternest was the man
Whose conscience most aggrieved him.

        " To this Ford
Thou cam'st the first, old comrade ! choice of arms
Is therefore thine by right ; " Cuchullain spake.
Ferdia chose the javelin.   Arrow-swift,
While still the charioteers brought back the shaft,
The missiles flew.   Keen-eyed as ocean bird
That, high in sunshine poised, glimpses his prey
Beneath the wave, and downward swooping slays him,
Each watched the other's movements, if an arm
Lifted too high, or buckler dropped too low,
Left bare a rivet.   Long that fight endured.
Three times exhausted sank their hands ; three times
They sat on rocks for respite, each the other
Eying askance, not silent : " Lo the man
Who shields an ox-like or a swine-like race
That strikes no blow itself ! " or thus : " Ah, pledge
Of amity eterne in old time sworn !
Ferdia, vow thy vow henceforth to maids !
The man-race nothing heeds thee ! "

Evening fell,
And stayed perforce that combat.    Slowly drew
The warriors near ; and, as they noted, each,
The other bleeding, friendship unextinct
In all its strength returned ; round either's neck
That other wound his arms and kissed him thrice.
That night their coursers in the self-same field
Grazed, side by side ; that night their charioteers
With rushes gathered from the self-same stream
Made smooth their masters' beds, then sat themselves
By the same fire.    Cuchullain sent the half
Of every healing herb that lulled his wounds
To staunch Ferdia's ; while to him in turn
Ferdia sent whate'er of meats or drinks
Held strengthening power or cordial, to allay
Distempered nerve or nimble spirit infuse,
In equal portions shared.
                            The second morn
They met at sunrise.    " Thine the choice of arms."
The Firbolg spake.    The Gael made answer, "Spears !"
Then leaped the champions on their battle-cars
And launched them into battle.    Dire their shock,
In fiery orbits wheeling now ; anon,
Wheel locked in wheel.    Profounder wounds by far
That day than on the first the warriors gored,
Since closer was the fight.    With laughing lip
Not less that eve Cuchullain sang the stave
That chides in war " Fomorian obstinacy."
Again at eve drew near they, slower now
For pain, and interwove fraternal arms ;

Again their coursers in the self-same field
Grazed side by side, and from the self-same stream
Again their charioteers the rushes culled ;
Again they shared alike both meats and drinks ;
Again those herbs allaying o'er their wounds
With incantations laid.

                Forlorn and sad
Peered the third morning o'er the vaporous woods,
The wan grey river with its floating weed
And bubble unirradiate.   From the marge
Cuchullain sadly marked the advancing foe :
" Alas, my brother ! beamless is thine eye ;
The radiance lives no longer on thy hair ;
And slow thy step."   The doomed one answered calm :
" Cuchullain, slow of foot but strong of hand
Fate drags his victim to the spot decreed.
The choice to-day is mine ; I choose the sword."

   So spake the Firbolg ; and they closed in fight ;
And straightway from his heart to arm and hand
Rushed up the strength of all that buried race
By him so loved !   Once more it swelled his breast,
Re-clothed in majesty each massive limb,
And flashed in darksome light of hair and eye,
Resplendent as of old.   Surpassing deeds
They wrought, while circled meteor-like their swords,
Or fell like heaven's own bolt on shield or helm.
Long hours they strove, till morning's purer gleam
Vanished in noon.   Sharper that day their speech ;
For, in the intenser present, years gone by
Hung but like pallid, thin horizon clouds

O'er memory's loneliest limit.   Evening sank
Upon the dripping groves and shuddering flood,
With rainy wailings.   Not as heretofore
Their parting.   Haughtily their mail they tossed,
Each to his followers.   In the self-same field
That night their coursers grazed not ; neither sat
Their charioteers beside the self-same fire ;
Nor sent they, each to other, healing herbs.

    Ere morn the Firbolg drank the strength of dreams,
Picturing his race's wrong ; and trumpet blasts
Went o'er him, blown from fields of ancient wars ;
And thus he mused, half-wakened : " Not for Meave ;
Not for the popular suffrage ; not for her,
That maid who fain had held me from the snare,
Fight I that fight whose end shall crown this day.
O race beloved, this day your vengeance dawns
Red in the East !   The mightiest of the Gaels
Goes down before me !   What if both should die?
So best !   Thus too the Firbolg is avenged ! "
So mused he.   Stately from his couch he rose,
And armed himself, sedate.   Upon his breast
He laid, in iron sheathed, a huge, flat stone,
For thus he said : " Though many a feat of arms
Is mine, from Scatha learned, or else self-taught,
The Gae-Bulg is Cuchullain's ! "   On his head
He fixed his helm, and on his arm his shield,
Sable as night, with fifty bosses bound,
All brass ; the midmost like a noontide sun.

    Cuchullain eyed him as he neared the Ford,
And spake to Leagh : " This day, if thou shouldst
    mark

This hand or slack or sluggish, hurl, as wont,
Sharp storm of arrowy railing from thy lips,
That so the battle-anger from on high
May flame on me." The choice of arms was his.
He chose "the Ford-Feat." On the Firbolg's brow
A shadow fell : — "All weapons there," he mused,
" Have place alike ; if on him falls the rage,
He will not spare the Gae-Bulg ! "
                                    Well they knew,
Both warriors, that the fortunes of that day
Must end the conflict ; that for one, or both,
The sun that hour ascending shone his last.
Therefore all strength of onset till that hour
By either loosed or hoarded, craft of fight
Reined in one moment but to spring the next
Forward in might more terrible, compared
With that last battle, was a trivial thing ;
Whilst every weapon, javelin, spear, or sword,
Lawful alike that day, scattered abroad
Huge flakes of dinted mail ; from every wound
Bounded the life-blood of a heart athirst
For victory or for death. The vernal day
Panted with summer ardours, while aloft
Noontide, a fire-tressed Fury, waved her torch,
Kindling the lit grove and its youngling green
From the azure-blazing zenith. Waxed the heat : —
So waxed the warriors' frenzy. Hours went by.
That day they sought not rest on rock or mound,
Held no discourse. Slowly the sun declined ;
And as wayfarers tired, when twilight falls,

Advance with strength renewed, so they, refreshed,
Surpassed their deeds at morning.   With a bound
Cuchullain, from the bank high springing, lit
Full on the broad boss of Ferdia's shield,
His dagger-point down turned.   With spasm of arm
Instant the Firbolg from its sable rim
Cast him astonished.   Upward from the Ford
Again Cuchullain reached that shield; again
With spasm of knee Ferdia flung him far,
While Leagh in scorn reviled him : " As the flood
Shoots on the tempest's blasts its puny foam,
The oak-tree casts its dead leaf on the wave,
The mill-wheel showers its spray, the shameless woman
Hurls on the mere that babe which was her shame, —
So hurls Ferdia forth that fairy-child
Whom men misdeemed for warrior ! "

        Then from heaven
Came down upon Cuchullain, like the night,
The madness-wrath.   The Foes confronted met ;
Shivered their spears from point to haft ; their swords
Flashed lightnings round them.   Fate-compelled, their
   feet
Drew near, then reached, that stream which backward
   fled,
Leaving its channel dry.   While raged that fight,
Cuchullain's stature rose, huge bulk, immense,
Ascending still ; as high Ferdia towered,
Like Fomor old or Nemed from the sea, —
Those shields — their covering late from foot to helm —
Shrinking, so seemed it, till above them beamed

Shoulders and heads.   So close that fight, their crests,
That waved defiance, mingled in mid air;
While all along the circles of their shields
And all adown their swords, ran, mad with rage,
Viewless for speed, the demons of dark moors
And war-sprites of the valleys, Bocanachs
And Banacahs, whose scream, so keen its edge,
Might shear the centuried forest as the scythe
Shears meadow grass.   To these in dread response
Thundered far off, from sea-caves billow-beat
And halls rock-vaulted 'neath the eternal hills,
That race Tuatha, giant once, long since
To pigmy changed, that forge from molten ores
For aye their clanging weapons, shield or spear,
On stony anvils, waiting the day decreed
Of vengeance on the Gael.   That tumult scared
The horses of the host of Meave, that brake
From war-car or the tethering rope, and spread
Ruin around.   Camp-followers first, then chiefs
Innumerable, were dragged along, or lay
'Neath broken axle, dead.   The end was nigh.
Cuchullain's shield, splintered upon his arm,
Served him no more ; and through his fenceless side
Ferdia drave the sword.   Then first the Gael
Hurled forth this taunt : "The Firbolg, bribed by
        Meave,
Has sold his ancient friend !"   Ferdia next,
" No Firbolg he, that man in Scatha's Isle,
Who won a maid, then left her !"   Backward stepped
Cuchullain paces three ; he reached the bank ;

He uttered low, "The Gae-Bulg!"   Instant, Leagh
Within his hand had lodged it.   Bending low,
Low as that stream — the war-game's crowning feat —
He launched it on Ferdia's breast.   The shield,
The iron plate beneath, the stone within it,
Like shallow ice-films 'neath a courser's hoof,
Burst.   All was o'er.   To earth the warrior sank;
Dying, he spake : " Not thine this deed, O friend ;
'Twas Meave who winged that bolt into my heart ! "
   Then ran Cuchullain to that great one dead,
And raised him in his arms, and laid him down
Beside the Ford, but on its northern bank,
Not in that realm by Ailill swayed and Meave.
Long time he looked the dead man in the face ;
Then by him fell in swoon.   "Cuchullain, rise !
The men of Erin be upon thee !   Rise ! "
Thus Leagh.   He answered, waking, " Let them come !
To me what profit if I live or die?
The man I loved is dead ! "
                              But by the dead
Cuchullain stood ; and thus he made lament :
" Ferdia !   On their head the curse descend,
Who sent thee to thy death !   We meet no more ;
Never while sun, and moon, and earth endure.
   " Ferdia !   Far away in Scatha's Isle
A great troth bound us, and a vow life-long,
Never to raise war-weapons, each on each.
'Twas Finobar that snared thee !   She shall die.
   " Ferdia ! dearer to my heart wert thou
Than all beside, if all were joined in one.

Dear was thy clouded face and darksome eye ;
Thy deep, sad voice ; thy words so wise and few ;
Dear was thy silence ; dear thy slow, grave ways,
Not boastful like the Gael's."

                 Silent he stood,
While Leagh in reverence from the dead man's breast
Loosened his mail.  There shone the torque of Meave ;
There, where the queen had fixed it, yet it lay.
Cuchullain clutched it.  " Ha ! that torque I spurned !
Dark gem ill-lifted from the seas of Death !
Swart planet bickering from the heavens of Fate !
With what a baleful beam thou look'st on me !
'Twas thou, 'twas thou, not I, that slew'st this man "—
He dashed it on the rock, and with his heel
Crushed it to fragments.

              Then, as one from trance
Waking, once more he spake : " O me — O me !
That I should see that face so great and pale !
To-day face-whitening death is on that face ;
And in my hand my sword ; — 'tis crimson yet.
That day, when he and I triumphed in fight
By Formait's lake o'er Scatha's pirate foes,
The woman fetched a beaker forth of wine,
And made us drink it both ; and made us vow
Friendship eterne.  O friend, my hand this day
Tendered a bloody beaker to thy lip."

   Again he sang : " Queen Meave to Uladh's bound
Came down ; and dark the deed that grew thereof ;
Came down with all the hosting of her kings ;
And dark the deed that grew thereof.  We two

Abode with Scatha in her northern Isle,
Her pupils twinned.   The sea-girt warrioress,
That honoured few men, honoured us alike ;
We ate together of the self-same dish ;
We couched together 'neath the self-same shield ;
Now living man I stand, and he lies dead !"
  He raised again his head ; once more he sang :
" Each battle was a game, a jest, a sport,
Till came, fore-doomed, Ferdia to the Ford ;
I loved the warrior though I pierced his heart.
Each battle was a game, a jest, a sport,
Till stood, self-doomed, Ferdia by the Ford, —
Huge lion of the forestry of war,
Fair, central pillar of the House of Fame !
But yesterday he towered above the world ;
This day he lies along the earth, a shade."


## IV

SILENCE amid the wide, confederate camp ;
No clang of sword or shield ; no warrior's tread,
Striding to Meave, with battle-gage down flung
For him who kept the Ford.   But when six days
Were past, and none had seen that threatening helm,
There went abroad a rumour, " He is dead."

  .   .   .   .   .   .   .   .   .   .   .

  Six days, and in Cuchullain's cell no change.
The bud grew large ; the earlier violet died ;
He neither spake nor moved.   His wounds were
    deep ;

E

Deeper his grief; for that cause ampler power
They gained, that clan accursed of Cailitin,
With ghostly spells darkening the warrior's heart.
As lie the dead, he lay.

                One eve, what time
The setting sun levelled through holly brakes
Unnumbered dagger-points of jewelled light,
And 'neath the oak-stem burned a golden spot,
Leagh, standing near his couch, reproached him thus :
" In time of old the greatness of thy spirit
Had ever strength to salve thy corporal griefs ;
But now through coward heart thou makest no fight,
Dying as old men die."   Cuchullain heard ;
But answered nought.

              Next day, while near them buzzed
At noon the gilded insect swarm, with sound
That stung the fever in his nerves, he spake :
" While lived Ferdia, wounds to thee were jest ;
Thy grief it is that drags thee to the pit ;
Grief ; and for what?   Of treasons worse is none
Than sorrow when thy country's foe is dead !
Not man is he, the man who dies of grief."
He spake ; Cuchullain fixed a vacant eye
On that sad, wrathful face.

            Then hastened Leagh
To where those giant coursers, side by side,
Stood tethered 'mid green grass and meadow-sweet
Within a lawn ; and led them to a stream,
And bade them drink ; and later led them home ;
And placed their corn before them, and they ate.

Next spake he : " Horses ye : and yet ye know
To eat at need, while men self-sentenced starve ! "
Thus of that man whom most he loved on earth
He made complaint.   Liath, the lake's white son,
Tossed high his head in anger.   By his side
Sangland, his dusky comrade, sadly ate,
Moistening with tears her barley.

                            Late that eve
Cuchullain beckoned Leagh : " To Conor speed.
Speak thus : ' Put on thine arms and save thy land,
Since now the Hound that kept thy gate is dead.
Make no delay ! ' "   At midnight Leagh went forth,
Though loth to leave his master to the care
Of cowherd rude, or swineherd.   Tenderer aid
Ere long consoled him.   Beauteous as the dawn,
Next morn, two shepherd boys, seeking a lamb,
Came on the sick man in his forest nook.
Long time they gazed on him compassionate ;
With voice benign and tendance angel-like
Onward into his confidence they crept ;
His lips with milk, the purest, they refreshed ;
They placed the dewy wood-flowers in his hand ;
They sang him ballads old, not battle-songs —
Too loud such songs they deemed — but Fairy lore,
Or tale of lovers fleeing tyrant's rage ;
Among the last unwittingly they sang
" Cuchullain's Wooing ; " how the youth had found
Eimer, the loveliest lady of the land
Within her bowery pleasaunce, girt with maids
Harping, or broidering fair in scarf deep-dyed

Blossom or bird ; how long he sued ; and how
She answered, " Woo my sister : woo not me ! "
How, glorying in her loveliness, her sire
Had sworn no chief should ever call her wife,
Who won her not by valour ; how that youth
Had scaled his rock, and slain his guards, and forth,
Through all the blazing ruins of that keep,
Led her by hand, a downward-looking bride,
Majestic, unconsenting, undismayed,
But likewise unreluctant.   As they sang
Above that suffering face there passed a smile ;
And where that smile had lain there crept a tear ;
And, in few minutes more, asleep he sank,
Who had not slept nine days. . .


## V

        . . . THAT night in Uladh's camp
Was silence strange and dread.   By dying men
Sat men sore wounded.   Scornful of their foe
And burning for revenge, the North had spurned
Science of war, their boast, and left, death-strewn,
Full half their host.   Between their tents and Meave's,
All that long night, the buriers of the dead
Groped their sad way with red, earth-grazing torch,
Turning the white face up in search of friend,
Brother, or son.   But in the tent of Meave
Triumph ruled all ; a hundred spake at once,
Each man his deeds recounting.   Far apart
Sat Fergus ; on his brow alone was shade.

Righteous that vengeance ; but his country's blood
Gladdened not him.   Of those that marked him, some
Had reverence for his sadness ; lesser souls,
That long had hated, loathed the man that hour.
Sudden the din surceased.   Far other sound
Quelled it ; from Uladh's sorrowing camp it swelled,
A jubilant cry soaring from earth to heaven !
Then flashed the eyes of Fergus, and he cried :
" Cuchullain lives !   That sound is Uladh's shout,
What time the host he enters ! "   With a brow,
Gloomy as night, the queen replied : " 'Tis false !
We know that in that forest, months gone by,
Cuchullain perished ! "   Silent stood they long,
Listening.   At last rang out far different note,
As piteous as the first was full of joy,
A funeral *keen* world-wide.   Then cried the queen :
" Cuchullain lived !   Cuchullain lives no more !
Wounded and weak he came to aid his own ;
Too great such effort for a wasted frame.
That was Cuchullain's death-dirge ! "   Fierce she
        stood ;
Glorying she spake ; and with attendance passed
Forth from the hall of banquet to her tent ;
But, as she passed, she heard at either side —
She and her ladies with her — trembling heard,
Swift as dead leaves by tempest borne o'er rocks,
The rushing of a panic-stricken host
Invisible, though now the dawn was grey, —
A host t'ward Shenan flying !   High o'er head
A dulcet strain, unutterably sad,

When ceased that phantom rush of fugitive feet,
Drifted far northward. Then the queen was ware
These were her country's gods that left her host.
The legend adds that in her tent that hour
Faythleen, the witch, she saw, who sat and wove
A mystic web and sang a mystic song,
Seen but by her :— and, later, o'er her bed
Men say that Orloff bent, her buried son,
And spake : " This day the battle shall be fought
Of Gairig and Ilgairig."

                         He, meanwhile,
The lord of all the battles, where was he,
Cuchullain? Many a weary day and week
Within his loved Murthemné's woods he lay,
Sore-wounded man, nigh death. Those shepherd
          youths
Tended him still, or sang beside his bed ;
And ofttimes o'er his face the tears of Leagh
In passionate gust descended. But the might
Unholy of the clan of Cailitin,
That nightly hung above him like a cloud,
Began to wither, when that mist accursed,
Which bound with Imbecility the land,
Drifted from Uladh's borders. On the breast
Pellucid, likewise, of Murthemné's streams
Benignant spirits scattered flowers and herbs,
With healing virtue dowered. He, morn and eve
In those clear currents laid, renewed his youth ;
And, pure as infant's, came again that flesh
Where festered late his wounds. At last, revived,

He passed, car-borne to Eman, north.   The fields
Devastated, and wail from foodless glens,
Filled him, as on he sped, with wrathful strength.
Next, tidings came of Conor's southward march :
Exultingly he followed.   On that night
Of overthrow he reached the royal camp.
Far off they kenned his car, and raised that shout
Heard never save for him.   When near he drew,
Way-worn and wearied, and around him gazed,
And  saw  that  sight,  and  thought,  "Too  late ;  too
    late ! "
His cheek down sank upon the breast of Leagh,
And all men deemed him dead.   Then rose that wail,
To Meave auspicious sound.

                               There are who deem
Cuchullain's tent that night was near the Well,
Where, purer far, more late the royal maids,
Fedelm and Ethna, met that saint, who gave
To God the isle of Fate.   Then, too, that Well
Blessing diffused, they say ; for from its brink
A runnel o'er the pebbles ran, with sound
So sweetly tuned that on the warrior sank
Deep seal of peace divine.   The war-shouts near,
To him thus harboured, seemed but ocean's sighs
Round islands ever calm.   Next came, on winds
Fresher than earth's, divinities more high,
He thought, than those that late from elfin meres
Amid Murthemné's woods had dewed his face ;
And loftier songs were sung ; and balmier flowers,
In holier fountains bathed, were softlier pressed

On bosom and brow; while shone before his eyes
Visions more fair than lordliest battle-field,
Though what they meant he knew not, nor divined —
High-towerèd temples cruciform, that rose
Far-seen o'er wood and street; and from their gates
Vestal procession issuing white, that wound
Through precincts low, where only dwelt the poor,
The halt, the lame, the blind; and song he heard,
With spiritual pathos changing sense to soul,   .
"The end of all is peace."   In silence slid
The constellations down the western sky;
And endless seemed the going of that night,
And measureless that joy.

                    At break of day
Came Conal Carnach and the Red Branch Knights
To see the sick man's face.   Thereon the dawn
Laughed, with glad beam; and, lo! where long had
      lain
Pallor of death, now burned a healthful red.
Not less they dared not touch him; since with him
*Geisa* it was, if any broke his rest.
They left him, and the battle-storm rang out.
Warned by defeat, Uladh had raised ere morn,
Fronting her camp, three bulwarks; at the first
And distant most, three hours the conflict raged.
It fell at last.   When rose the conquerors' shout,
Leagh to Cuchullain crept, and touched him not,
Yet knelt and whispered, "Heard you not that sound?"
And thus Cuchullain answered still in trance :
"I heard the runnels in Murthemné's woods,

Snow-swoll'n in spring." Then Leagh stood up and
    mused,
" The hue of health is on his face, and yet,
Because he will not wake, the land is shamed."
Next, round the second bulwark raged the war,
Hour after hour ; heroic deeds were done ;
Heroic deaths were died ; at last it fell ;
Again, and nearer, rose the conquerors' shout ;
Again, with bolder foot and forehead flushed,
Leagh to Cuchullain moved, and touched him not,
But, bending, murmured, " Heard you not that sound ? "
And he, without awaking, answered thus :
" I heard the birds in Eimer's pleasaunce sing,
Honouring our marriage morn." Then Leagh went
    forth
Groaning, and smote his hands, and wept aloud :
" Because he will not wake, the host must die ! "
Around the loftiest bulwark and the last
Once more for hours the battle raged ; it fell !
And louder thrice that shout went up. The gaze
Of Leagh was on him fixed ; he heard it not ;
Slowly it died ; and as it died the wail
Came feebly forth from Uladh's host. A wail,
Since those old days of Cullain and his hound,
To him was thrilling more than battle shout.
A change went o'er his face ; like fire it shone ;
Within his tent he stood, midway ! Then, lo !
A marvel ! for the wounded man, that slept
All day with bandages enswathed, up-towered
Full-armed for fight, a champion, spear in hand,

Work of some god !   Swift from his tent he strode.
Without the hand of man there stood his car,
And those immortal steeds, pawing the air,
Like shapes with pinions clad.   A moment more,
And forward to Ilgairig's slope they dashed.
" Let but the armies see him," inly mused
Leagh, "and the work is done ! "

                            Onward they sped ;
But not unnoted by that demon brood
That hate the works of justice.   From below,
Writhing in torment of their rage, they heaved
The grassy surface upward into waves,
Now swelling, now descending.   Strong albeit,
The immortal steeds staggered.   Cuchullain cried :
" What ! children of the tempest-wakened lakes,
Saw ye till now no billows ?   Yours they are !
To others fatal, they but fawn on you !
Exult ye in your native element,
And waft your lord to vengeance ! "   They obeyed ;
They reached Ilgairig's summit.

                          On he sped,
Mantled with sunset.   Terrible he shone !
Both armies saw him — knew him !   Onward yet ;
While from his golden arms and golden car
Lightnings went forth incessant.   In his van
Victory and Fear their pinions spread.   He reached
Ilgairig's southern verge ; he reined his steeds ;
High in his car he stood ; with level hand
Screening his eyes, he scanned that battle-field,
His future course decreeing.

On and on
Adown that slope he flashed and o'er that plain
Like zigzag sunshaft o'er the autumnal world ;   .
And ever where he came the host of Meave
Gave way before him.   On and ever on !
And now the nearest of those bulwarks three
He reached, and o'er its ruins swept, back driving
The conquerors late, now conquered.   On and on !
And ever through that foe, thick-packed, he clave
A lane of doom and death.   Ere long they reached
The second rampart.   There it was he slew
The great ones of Clan Libna, and the clans
Guairé and Murdoc.   Fiery faces thronged
The air around him, and the voice of Gods
Made smooth his way triumphant.

On and on !
Nor ceased he ever hurling left and right
Destruction from his sling ; nor slackened sleet
Of javelins winged with fate.   That brazen urn,
With death-stones heaped, exhausted not its store,
Replenished ever as by hand unseen ;
Work of some God !   That brazen cirque, not less,
Where stood his javelins ranged, was never void ;
Work of some God !   The on-rolling wheels de-
       voured
Those serried ranks ; the war-steeds trampled down.
Reached was that rampart furthest of the three.
There in her war-car sat the queen ; in front
The Maineys Seven were ranged ; his sword forth
       flashed ;

Four perished of the seven.   Then faced the queen
Westward, and fled amazed.
                    He marked her flight ;
Eastward he turned.   As on he carved his course,
Not now a lane alone of doom and death
But ever widening valleys ruin-strewn
Bore witness of his transit, for behind
Closed ever up Cuchullain's household clans,
Murthemné's and Cuailgné's.   Perished there
The Ossorians, and the Olnemacian chiefs,
And many a champion famed from Slaney's bank
To Lee and Laune, from Caiseal's crested rock
To Beara's strand.   Who died not, fled, and left
Yet ampler, 'twixt the bristling flanks of war,
That vacant space ; and as the dolphin oft,
Raptured by gladness of clear summer seas
While flames the noon on purple billows, swims
All round and round some ship full-sailed, — so he
Circled on foot at times that car wind-swift,
Mocking its slowness ; then, with airy bound,
Once more within it beamed.   His boyhood's mirth
Returned upon him.   On the chariot's floor
He marked those brazen balls — the sport that time
Of men way-faring — snatched them up, tossed high,
While yet careering round the blood-stained field,
Then caught them as they fell — a glittering ring
They girt that glittering head.   Not less his eye,
Watchful, pursued the flying foe ; his hand
Brought down to earth the fleetest.
                      From the crests

Of those twinned hills down rushed the total strength,
At last, of Uladh.   Universal flight
Shook the vast field.   The bravest men and best,
Caught by its current, on were dragged like trees,
The sport of winter flood.   Chieftain and king
Sought, each, his home.  Meave, with a remnant small.
Reached  Shenan's  bridgeless  tide ;   and  there  had
     fallen,
Stretching to towered Ath-Luain helpless hands,
Save that Cuchullain, 'mid the narrower way
Standing with arms extended, terrible,
Abashed that host pursuing : " Stand ye back !
One day I shared her feast ; she shall not die ! "
He spake, and set by Shenan's wave his shield.
Next morn the Ulidians, where that shield had stood,
In silence stern planted three pillar-stones,
White daughters of the tempest-beaten hills,
In Ogham graved, " Vanquished by Uladh's sons,
Here fled the invader, Meave."
                              Fergus alone,
The Exile-King, and they, the Exile Band,
Fled not that day.   Though few, and bleeding fast,
Fearless upon a cloudy crag they stood,
Phalanx prepared to die, prepared not less
Dearly to sell their lives, while past them streamed
That panic-stricken throng.   The host pursuing
Looked up, yet swerved not from their course.   Once
     more,
Returning from the vengeance, they looked up ;
Then passed, in silence, by.

                              That eve, men say,
While slowly paced Cuchullain t'ward the camp,
Bosomed 'twixt Gairig's and Ilgairig's hills,
Lamenting strains of Goddesses were heard —
For whatsoe'er was female loved the man,
If earthly female, with a human love,
If heavenly, with a love compassionate —
Lamenting strains, that, ere his youth had passed,
That starry head must lie, by Fate's decree,
Amid the dust of death.   Cuchullain turned ;
Softly he answered : " Goddesses benign !
Why weep ye?   I was Uladh's Mastiff-Hound :
The mastiff lives not long.   What better lot
For him than this ; — the bandits chased, to die
Beside his master's gate ? "

*The maiden, DEIRDRÉ, at whose birth it had been prophesied that she should bring destruction upon ULADH, lived secluded in an island, by the will of CONOR, the King, who destined her for himself. There she heard the fame of the Three Heroes, the SON OF USNACH, whose fate she was. The following passage relates her meeting with NAISI, eldest of the Three.*

ONE day it chanced that, while the March wind's
    breath
Was softening round the daffodil's first bud,
Their shepherd old had saved a lamb from death,
    And slain the wolf, and in their gateway stood ;
And, as the wounded creature bled, below
A crimson blood-pool stained the last night's snow.

Sudden, there swooped to earth a raven black,
    And feasted on that blood.   As in a dream
The maiden watched it long : at last she spake,
    Whilst o'er her grave face ran a laughing gleam :
"These be Love's colours, black, and red, and white ;
Yet love, we know, is nought, when judged aright !

"These be Love's colours, white, and black, and red.
    Some little foolish maid, to love inclined,
Might say : 'Though all should love me, none shall wed,
    Until in one dear face those three I find ;
Not raven locks alone, or front of snow,
But on the heroic cheek the battle's glow !'"

Beside the girl stood Levarcam ; she smiled,
    And spake : " Good sooth, your shaft hath hit its
         mark ;
Yea, doubtless, you were born a prophet's child !
    For Naisi's front is white, his tresses dark ;
And still of him men say, ' On Naisi's cheek
Not roses, but red dawns of battles break ! ' "


Then to the flash from Deirdré's peerless eyes
    Her nurse made answer : " Naisi ! who is he ?
Warrior there treads not under Erin's skies
    But knows the man, — the swiftest of those Three !
No hounds they need ; alone they chase, each morn,
The stag, and downward drag him head and horn !


" Ever at Uladh's feasts the clansmen say, —
    ' Place ye the sons of Usnach side by side,
A rock behind them, or some cromlech grey ;
    Then blow a trump o'er Erin, far and wide,
And range her hosts against them, face to face, —
Those Three shall hew them down, and homeward
         chase ! '


" Their singing is the best all Uladh boasts ;
    Of all her sons most courteous they and kind ;
To heaven devoutest of her countless hosts ;
    Softly along his path they lead the blind ;
Submission made, no more remember ill,
Nor ever kissed a maid against her will.

" To these the clans send embassies from far
   Laden with gifts, and suing, ' Grant us aid !
Rule us in battle's hour, and head our war ! '
   But women say, ' How well their mother prayed
For sons both mild and valiant ! '   Lo, a ray
Of her sweet countenance lives in theirs this day ! "


Here Levarcam a moment stopped for breath ;
   Then Deirdré rose and sought the neighbouring
      strand ;
Ice-bound it was, and cold that hour as death, —
   To her 'twas warm as mead by May breeze fanned ;
She paced along its pebbly beach for hours,
And to her feet its shingles felt like flowers.


Returned, more lofty looked she than at morn ;
   With more of inward gladness, yet less gay ;
More confident, though lost her girlish scorn
   In some half womanhood's benigner ray ;
Smiling, she met her nurse's smile, and then,
" Naisi," she said, "will love me !  Who cares when ? "


The maiden paused ; she mused ; again she spake,
   Fixing on Levarcam those marvellous eyes :
" Three be Love's colours — white, and red, and black :
   White, for the sake of Love's white sanctities ;
And red, for Love must war on many a foe ;
And black, since Love, though crowned, must end in
      woe."

F

Again she mused : — "Yes, Love must war ! Who
　　　fears ?
Though Love must fight, he fights in love, not hate !
Some glorious conflict rages through the years ;
　　　Great Love must take therein his part, elate.
And woe comes last.　On raven pinions borne
Night comes not less ; but after night comes morn !"


From that time Naisi's name she named no more ;
　　　Nothing she seemed to lack, nothing to crave ;
Her heart through spiritual realms was strong to soar,
　　　Self-lifted, as from windless seas the wave ;
A spirit of strength from earthly bonds escaped,
She trod, — her body's self but spirit draped ; —


A spirit of strength and swiftness onward borne
　　　Through luminous realms all resonant and free,
Happier because unwinged, like endless morn
　　　With silver feet circling the sphèred sea ;
And still her lonely thought with song was blent ;
And, bird-like, still she warbled as she went.


For music then, like warfare, not from art
　　　Grew up laborious ; born of frank good-will,
'Twas Joy's loud clarion in the generous heart ;
　　　Through pains more perfect grew the harper's skill ;
Yet still, from purest soul and noblest breast,
The minstrelsy, perforce, became the best.

Deirdré, besides, on Naisi's music musing —
    That strain far-famed she once had heard in dream —
Through some strange craft of Nature's sweet infusing
    Unconscious, copied it.   A lily's gleam
Shines thus, reflected in the lake below,
More softly, green for green, and snow for snow.


Once, too, she marked two mated eagles flying
    Far from their cliff, her little lake above,
Sunward in strength, and clapped her hands loud
        crying, —
    " On, wedded Spirits, on ! for this is Love !
No woodland murmurs yours, and thraldom none !
Sail on till buried in the ascending sun ! "


That vision shaped her life.  Through wild and wood
    Long hours that morn had Naisi chased the stag.
It took the wave and vanished.  Silent stood,
    At noon, the hunter on a jutting crag ;
His eye upon a tower-crowned island fell ;
Thereon it fastened, bound as by a spell.


" There lies," he mused, " that wondrous-countenanced
       child,
    Like some poor bird a captive from its birth,
In that lone island, year by year, exiled.
    How little she suspects her grace and worth !
Our household foe, ere long, will clutch that hand —
Is yon a causeway leading to the land? "

An hour had fled, and lo ! that bridge he paced.
    Ere long, no child, but, sparkling like a flower,
The imprisoned maid, nor startled nor shame-faced,
    Passed by the youth, advancing from her bower
With breeze-like step, yet down-dropped lids of snow :
" Ah foot," he cried, " more light than foot of doe ! "


An instant back she flashed her magic eyes,
    And from her laughing lip the answer leaped :
" Where stags are none, the doe must monarchise ! "
    Some ballad old it was, but never steeped
Till then with such strange sweetness to his ear.
Was it reproof or challenge, vague yet dear ?


Naisi rejoined : " A monarch rules this land ;
    For you he destines Erin's proudest throne !
Ah, but for that how many a warrior's brand " —
    " His realm," she said, " is his ; my heart mine own.
A maiden I have lived ; maiden would die."
The warrior fixed on hers his strong grey eye.


That eye, though young and sweet with such clear
        light,
    Had marshalled many a death-strewn battle-field ;
Had watched the meeting tides of many a fight ;
    Taught many a proud, inviolate fort to yield.
With gaze as frank and clear thus answered she, —
" I know you well ! the eldest of those Three !

" Where are your brothers? She, whom nurse I call,
   Has told me all the Three are kind and brave.
Fain would I sister be to each and all ;
   Fain, too, my life from love tyrannic save ! "
" Their sister you shall be," the youth replied ;
" Mine if you will ; but, none the less, my bride ! "

He spake ; then, for the maiden's safety fearing,
   With passion changed, continued : " Spurn my suit !
The king will slay thee ! " She, the warrior nearing,
   Held forth both hands, and gazed upon him mute ;
And last, in love's high truth — and truth is best —
Made answer, " Thine ! " He snatched her to his
     breast.

Thence lifting soon a countenance glad yet tearful,
   She spake : " Your knighthood stands consummate
     now !
Since a true maid, of Conor's wrath not fearful,
   Has heard, and with her own has crowned your vow.
Forth, on your task decreed ! Fly hence, and prove
Ten years in battle-fields what might hath Love !

" In ten years bring me back your trophied spoils
   From every land and clime ; for mine they are !
I, that inspired, can well requite your toils ;
   Ever till then, my spirit like a star
O'er you shall hang ! Farewell ! yet, ere you go,
Sing ! for how great your songs, long since I know."

So, hand in hand, upon that causeway standing,
  Those youthful lovers measure after measure
Poured forth, their bosoms more and more expanding
  At once with music's zeal and love's pure pleasure ;
For Deirdré still her voice with Naisi's twined,
All-perfect harmony though undesigned.

●

And though till then no war-song she had sung,
  That hour her song grew warlike as his own ;
And, o'er her heaven-like beauty as he hung,
  His war-songs tender grew, and sweet of tone ;
And still they sang, till now, through woods loud ring-
        ing,
The men of Erin, east and west, came winging,


And found those lovers in that lonely haunt, —
  That sunset round them glowing and above ;
And saw the forests flash, the blue waves pant ;
  And heard that mingled praise of war and love.
Then ceased that pair, and softly smiled, and said, —
" What makes us glad is this : we two are wed ! "


But when, to many a questioner replying,
  They found that they had only met that noon,
The lovers laughed a sweet-voiced laughter, crying, —
  " We thought we had been wedded many a moon !
Great love, it seems, lives long in little time ;
Yet shall great love be ever in his prime !

" Perchance of us some future bard shall say, —
 'Their bright, swift life went o'er them like a breath
Of stormy southwind in the merry May ;
 And brief their unfeared, undivided death : '
For unto those who love, and love aright,
Life is Love's day ; and Death his long, sweet night."

But straight the men of Erin cried aloud, —
 "'The king, the king !'" and Naisi's brothers twain,
Ainli and Ardan, though to help him vowed
 At need, not less to break that troth were fain ;
" Beware," they cried ; " since Cathbad long ago
Foretold that Babe was born for Uladh's woe !"

Yet, when within those lovers' eyes they saw
 Wild mirth alone, and blank astonishment,
They deemed the thing divine ; and, though with awe,
 Their spirits on the high adventure bent,
And council took, and with one mind decreed
That self-same night o'er Uladh's bound to speed.

This therefore was the order of their going :
 A hundred warriors marching in the van ;
A hundred maidens next with veils loose flowing ;
 A hundred clansmen last, of Usnach's clan,
And each a greyhound leading in a cord ;
Swiftly with these they trod the moonlit sward.

# THE CHILDREN OF LIR

DEUS DEDIT CARMINA IN NOCTE. JOB XXXV. 10

## CANTO I ·

### THE STEPMOTHER'S MALEDICTION

ERE yet great Miledh's sons to Erin came,
 Lords of the Gael, Milesian styled more late,
An earlier tribe — Tuatha was their name,
 Likewise Dedannan — ruled the Isle of Fate ;
A tribe that knew nor clan, nor priest, nor bard,
Wild as the waves, and as the sea-cliffs hard.


Some say that race of old from Greece exiled
 Long time had sojourned in the frozen North,
Roaming Norwegian wood and Danish wild ;
 To Erin thence more late they issued forth,
And thither brought two gifts both loved and feared,
The Lia Fail, and Ogham lore revered.


Fiercer they were, not manlier, than the Gael ;
 Large-handed, swift of foot, dark-haired, dark-eyed,
With sudden gleams athwart their faces pale,
 Transits of fancies swift, or angry pride ;
Strange lore they boasted, imped by insight keen,
Blackened at times by gusts of causeless spleen.

These, when the white fleet of the Gael drew nigh
    Green Erin's shore — their heritage decreed —
O'er-meshed, through rites unholy, earth and sky
    With sudden gloom.   The invaders took no heed,
But dashed through dark their galleys on the strand ;
Then clapped their hands, and laughing leaped to land.


Around them drew Tuatha's race in guile,
    Unarmed, with mocking voice and furtive mien,
And scoffed : " Not thus your fathers fought erewhile !
    Say, call ye warriors knaves that creep unseen,
While true men sleep, up inlet dim and fiord,
Filching the land they proved not with their sword?"


Then to the Gael their bard, Amergin, spake :
    " Sail forth, my sons, nine waves across the deep,
And, when this island-race are armed, come back ;
    Take then their realm by force ; and, taking, keep !"
The Gael sailed forth, nine waves ; then turned, and
        gazed —
Night wrapt the isle, and storm by magic raised !


Round Erin's shores like leaves their ships were blown ;
    Strewn on her reefs lay bard and warrior drowned ;
Not less the Gael upreared ere long that throne,
    Two thousand years through all the West renowned.
O'er Taillten's field God held the scales of Fate ;
That last dread battle closed the dire debate.

There fell those three Tuatha queens who gave
 The land their names — they fell by death dis-
  crowned ;
There many a Gaelic chieftain found his grave ;
 Thenceforth the races twain adjusted bound
And right, at times by league, at times by war ;
Nor any reigned as yet from shore to shore.


Still, here and there, Tuatha princes ruled,
 Now in green vale, and now on pale blue coast, —
A warrior one, and one in magic schooled ;
 The graver made Druidic lore their boast,
And knew the secret might of star and leaf ;
Grey-haired King Bove stood up of these the chief.


Southward by broad Lough Derg his palace stood ;
 Northward, beside Emania's lonely mere,
In Finnaha, embowered 'mid lawn and wood,
 King Lir abode, a warrior, not a seer ;
Well loved was he, plain man with great, true heart,
Who loathed, despite his race, the sorcerer's art.


Five centuries lived he ere that better light
 Gladdened the earth from Bethlehem ; ne'ertheless
He judged his land with justice and with might,
 Tempering the same at times with gentleness ;
And gave the poor their due ; and made proclaim, —
" Let no man smite the old ; the virgin shame."

His prime was spent in wars ; in middle life
    He bade a youthful princess share his throne ;
Nor e'er had monarch yet a truer wife,
    With tenderer palm or voice of sweeter tone.
The one sole lady of that race was she
Sun-haired, with large eyes azure as the sea.


She moved amid the crafty as a child ;
    Amid the lawless, chaste as unsunned maid ;
Amid the unsparing, as a turtle mild ;
    Wondering at wrong ; too gentle to upbraid ;
Yet many a fell resolve, as she rode by,
Died at its birth — the ill-thinker knew not why !


Sadness before her fled.   In years long past,
    As on a cliff the warriors sang their songs,
A harper maid, with eyes that stared aghast,
    Had chaunted, — " Not to us this isle belongs !
The Fates reserve it for a race more true,
Ye children of Dedannan's stock, than you ! "


And, since she scorned her music to abate,
    Nor ceased to freeze their triumph with her dirge,
The princes and the people rose in hate,
    And hurled her harp and her into the surge ;
Yet still, halfway 'twixt midnight and the morn,
    That dirge swelled up, by tempest onward borne !

Remembering oft this spectre of his youth,
    King Lir would sit, a frown upon his brow ;
Then came the queen with words of peace and truth :
    " Mourn they that sinned !   A child that hour wert
        thou !
Thou rul'st this land to-day ; in years to be
Who best deserves shall wield her sovereignty."


Then would the monarch doff his sullen mood
    With kingly joy, and, bright as May-day's morn,
Ride forth amid his hounds through wild and wood,
    Thrilling far glens with echoes of his horn ;
Or meet the land's invaders face to face,
Well pleased, and homeward hew them with disgrace.


Thus happy lived the pair, and happier far
    When four fair children graced the royal house,
Fairer than flowers, more bright than moon or star
    Shining through vista long of forest boughs :
Finola was the eldest, eight years old ;
The yearling, Conn, best loved of all that fold.


These beauteous creatures with their mother shared
    Alike her blissful nature and sweet looks,
Like her swan-soft, swan-white, blue-eyed, bright-
        haired,
    With voices musical as birds or brooks ;
Beings they seemed reserved for some great fate,
Mysterious, high, elect, and separate.

At times they gambolled in the sunny sheen ;
    At times, Fiacre and Aodh at her side,
Finola paced the high-arched alleys green,
    At once their youthful playmate and their guide ;
A mother-hearted child she walked, and pressed
That infant, daily heavier, to her breast.


Great power of Love, that, wide as heaven, dost brood
    O'er all the earth, and doest all things well !
Light of the wise, and safeguard of the good !
    Nowhere, methinks, thou better lov'st to dwell
Than in the hearts of innocents that still,
By dangerous love untempted, work Love's will !


Thou shalt be with them when the sleet-wind blows
    Not less than in the violet-braided bower ;
Through thee 'mid desert sands shall bud the rose,
    The wild wave anthems sing !   In trial's hour
A germ of thine shall breed that quenchless Faith,
Amaranth of life, and asphodel of death.


Ah, lot of man !   Ah, world whose life is change !
    Ah, sheer descent from topmost height of good
To deepest gulf of anguish sudden and strange !
    A nation round their monarch's gateway stood ;
All day there stood they, whispering in great dread :
The herald came at last — " Our Queen is dead ! "

In silence still they stood, an hour and more,
  Till through the West had sunk the great red sun,
And from the castle wall and turrets hoar
  The latest crimson utterly had gone ;
At last the truth had reached them ; then on high
An orphaned People hurled its funeral cry.


They hurled it forth again, and yet again, —
  The dreadful wont of that barbaric time ;
Cry after cry, that reached the far-off main,
  And, echoing, seemed from cloud to cloud to
      climb ;
Then lifted hands like creatures broken-hearted,
Or sentenced men ; and homeward, mute, departed.


Fast-speeding Time, albeit the wounded wing
  He may not bind, brings us at least the crutch.
Winter was over, and the on-flying Spring
  Grazed the sad monarch's brow with heavenly touch,
And raised the head, now whitening, from the ground,
And stanched, not healed, the heart's eternal wound.


King Bove, chief sovereign of the dark-haired race,
  Sent to him saying, " Quit thee like a man !
The Gaels, our scourge, and Erin's sore disgrace,
  Advance, each day, their armies, clan by clan ;
Against them march thy host with mine, and take
To wife my daughter, for thy children's sake."

Lir sadly mused ; but answered : " Let it be ! "
   And drave with fifty chariots in array
To where the land's chief river like a sea,
   There named Lough Derg, spreads out in gulf and
      bay,
And many a woody mountain sees its face
Imaged in that clear flood with softened grace.


There with King Bove the widowed man abode
   Two days amid great feastings.   On the third
The king led forth his daughter — o'er her glowed
   A dim veil jewel-tissued — with this word :
" Behold thy wife !   The world proclaims her fair ;
I know her strong to love, and strong to dare."


And Lir made answer : " Fair she is as when
   A mist-veiled yew, red-berried, stands in state ;
Can love, you say !   Love she my babes ! and then
   With her my love shall bide ; if not — my hate."
And she, a crimson on her dusky brow,
Replied, — " If so it be, then be it so !"


King Lir, a fortnight more in revels spent,
   Made journey to his castle in the North
With her, his youthful consort, well content ;
   Arrived, in rapture of their loving mirth
Forth rushed into his arms his children four,
Bright as those wavelets on their blue lake's shore ;

On whom the new queen cast a glance oblique
   One moment's space ; then, flinging wide her arms,
With instinct changed, and impulse lightning-like,
   Clasped them in turn, and wondered at their charms,
And cried, — " If e'er a stepmother could love,
I of that tribe renowned will tenderest prove."


And so, by her great loving of those four,
   Still from her husband won she praises sweet,
And plaudits from his people, more and more ;
   Her own she called them ; nor was this deceit ;
She loved them with a fitful love — a will
To make them or to mar, for good or ill.


She wooed them still with shows, with flowers, with
      fruit ;
   Daily for them new sports she sought and found ;
Yet, if their father praised them, she was mute,
   And, when he placed them on his knee, she frowned,
Murmuring, — " How  blue  their  eyes !  their  cheek
      how pale !
Their voices too are voices of the Gael ! "


Meantime, as month by month in grace they grew,
   Their father loved them better than before ;
And so, one eve, their slender cots he drew
   Each from its place remote, and lightly bore,
And laid them ranged before his royal bed ;
And o'er the four a veil gold-woven spread, —

Their mother's bridal-veil ; and still, as dawn
    Was in its glittering tissue caged and caught,
He left his couch, and, that light veil withdrawn,
    Before his children stood in silent thought ;
And, if they slept, he kissed them in their sleep,
Then watched them with clasped hands in musings
        deep.


And, if they slept not, from their balmy nest
    With under-sliding arms he raised them high,
And clasped them each, successive, to his breast,
    Or on them flashed the first light from the sky ;
Then laid him by his mute, sleep-feigning bride,
And slept once more ; and oft in sleep he sighed.


Which things abhorring, she her face averse
    Turned all day steadfast from the astonished throng ;
And next, as one that broods upon a curse,
    She sat in her sick-chamber three weeks long,
And never raised her eyes, nor made complaint,
Dark as a fiend and silent as a saint.


Lastly to Lir she spake : "Daily I sink
    Downward to death. I wither in my prime ;
Home to my father I would speed, and drink
    Once more the breezes of my native clime ;
All night in sleep along Lough Derg I strayed,
And wings of strength about my shoulders played.

    G

" These four — *thy* children — with me I will take
    To please my father's eye ; he loves them well ;
Thou too, whene'er thy leisure serves, shalt make
    Thither thy journey."    All the powers of Hell
Thrilled at that speech in penal vaults below ;
But Lir, no fraud suspecting, answered, — " Go ! "


Therefore, next morn, when earliest sunrise smote
    Green mead to golden near the full-fed stream,
They caught four steeds, that grazed thereby remote,
    And yoked abreast beside the chariot-beam ;
And, when the sun was sinking toward the West,
By Darvra's lake drew rein, and made their rest.


Then the bad queen, descending, round her cast
    A baleful look of mingled hate and woe,
And with those babes into a thicket passed,
    And drew a dagger from her breast ; and, lo !
She struck them not, but only wailed and wailed —
In her so strongly womanhood prevailed.


The mood was changed.    She smiled that smile
      which none
    How wise soe'er, beholding, could resist,
And drew those children to her, one by one ;
    Then wailed once more, and last their foreheads
      kissed,
And cried with finger pointing to the lake, —
" Hence ! and in that clear bath your pastime take ! "

She spoke, and from their silken garb forth-sliding,
    Ere long those babes were sporting in the bay ;
And, as it chanced, the eddy past them gliding
    Wafted a swan's plume ; 'twas less white than they ;
Frowning, the queen beheld them, and on high
Waved thrice her Druid wand athwart the sky.


Then, standing on the marge, wan-cheeked, wide-
       eyed,
    As near they drew, awe-struck and wondering,
Therewith she smote their golden heads, and cried, —
    " Fly hence, ye pale-faced children of the king !
Cleave the blue mere, or on through ether sail ;
No more his loved ones, but a dolorous tale ! "


Straightway to snow-white swans those children turned ;
    And, sideway as they swerved, the creatures four
Fixed on her looks with human grief that yearned ;
    Then slowly drifted backward from the shore ;
While loud with voice unchanged, Finola cried, —
" Bad deed is thine, false queen and bitter bride !


" Bad deed, afflicting babes that harmed thee not ;
    Bad deed, and to thyself an evil dower ;
Disastrous more than ours shall be thy lot !
    Thou too shalt feel the weight of Druid power ;
From age to age thy penance ne'er shall cease ;
Our doom, though long it lasts, shall end in peace."

Then rang a wild shriek from that dreadful shape :
   " Long, long, ay long shall last those years of woe !
Here on this lake from misty cape to cape
   Three centuries ye shall wander to and fro ;
Three centuries more shall stem with heavier toil
Far Alba's waves, the black sea-strait of Moyle.


" Lastly three centuries, where the Eagle-Crest
   O'er-looks the western deep and Inisglaire,
Upon the mountain waves that know not rest
   Shall be your rolling palace, foul or fair,
Till comes the Tailkenn, sent to sound the knell
Of darkness, and ye hear his Christian bell."


Lo, as a band of lilies, white and tall,
   Beneath a breeze of morning bend their head,
High held in virgin state majestical,
   So meekly cowered those swans in holy dread,
Hearing that promised Tailkenn's blissful name !
For they long since had heard in dream the same.


Then fell a dew of meekness on the proud,
   Noting their humble heart ; and drooped her front;
And sorrow closed around her like a cloud ;
   And thus, with other voice than was her wont,
To those soft victims of her wrath she cried :
" Woe, woe !   Yet Fate must rule, whate'er betide !

"The deed is done; but thus much I concede:
　　In you the human heart shall never fail,
Changed though ye be and masked in feathery weed;
　　Your voice shall sweet remain as voice of Gael;
And all who hear your songs shall sink in trance,
And, sleeping, dream some great deliverance."


She spake, and smote her hands; and, at her word,
　　Once more the attendants caught the royal steeds
Grazing in peace beside the hornèd herd
　　Amid the meadow flowers and yellow weeds;
And fiercely through the night that dark one drave,
And reached Lough Derg, what time above its wave


The sun was rising; and at set of sun
　　Entered once more her father's palace gate;
Seated thereby, his nobles, every one,
　　Arose and welcomed her with loving state;
She answered naught, but sternly past them strode
And found her girlhood's bower, and there abode.


But when of Lir King Bove had made demand,
　　She answered thus: "Enough! My Lord is
　　　　naught;
Nor will he trust his children to thy hand,
　　Lest thou shouldst slay them." Long in silent
　　　　thought
The old man stood, then murmured in low tone,—
"I loved those children better than mine own!"

That night in dream King Lir had anguish sore,
    And southward, ere the dawn, rode far away
With many a chief to see his babes once more
    Beside Lough Derg ; and, lo ! at close of day,
Nighing to Darvra's lake, the westering sun
In splendour on the advancing horsemen shone.


Straightway from that broad water's central stream
    Was heard a clang of pinions and swift feet —
Unchanged at heart, those babes had caught that
        gleam ;
    Instant from far had rushed, their sire to greet,
Spangling the flood with silver spray ; and ere
That sire had reached the margin, they were there.


Then, each and all, clamorous they made lament,
    Recounting all their wrong, and all the woe ;
And Lir, their tale complete, his garments rent,
    Till then transfixed like marble shape ; and, lo !
Three   times,   heart-grieved,   that   concourse   raised
        their cry,
Piercing the centre of the low-hung sky.


But Lir knelt down upon the shining sand,
    And cried, — " Though great the might of Druid
        charms,
Return, and feel once more your native land,
    And find once more, and fill, your father's arms ! "
And they made answer : " Till the Tailkenn come,
We tread not land !   The waters are our home."

But when Finola saw her father's grief,
　　She added thus : " Albeit our days are sad,
The twilight brings our pain in part relief ;
　　And songs are ours by night that make us glad ;
Yea, each that hears our music, though he grieve,
Rejoices more.　Abide, for it is eve."


So Lir, and his, couched on the wave-lipped sod
　　All night ; and ever, as those songs up-swelled,
A mist of sleep upon them fell from God,
　　And healing Spirits converse with them held ;
And Lir was glad all night ; but with the morn
Anguish returned ; and thus he cried, forlorn :


" Farewell !　The morn is come ; and I depart.
　　Farewell !　Not wholly evil are things ill !
Farewell, Finola !　Yea, but in my heart
　　With thee I bide ; there liv'st thou changeless still ;
O Aodh ! O Fiacre ! the night is gone —
Farewell to both !　Farewell, my little Conn ! "


Southward the childless father rode once more,
　　And saw at last beyond the forests tall
The great lake and the palace on its shore ;
　　And, entering, onward passed from hall to hall
To where King Bove majestic sat and crowned,
High on a terrace with his magnates round ;

A stately terrace clustered round with towers,
   And jubilant with music's merry din,
Beaten by resonant waves, and bright with flowers ;
   There — but apart—she stood that wrought the sin,
Like one that broods on one black thought alone
Seen o'er a world of happy hopes o'erthrown.


The throng made way; onward the wronged one
      strode
   To Bove, sole-throned and lifting in his hand
For royal sceptre that Druidic rod
   Which gave him o'er the Spirit-world command ;
Then, pointing to that traitress, false as fair,
That wronged one spake : "There stands the mur-
      deress ! — there ! "


Straight on the King Druidic insight fell ;
   And, mirrored in his mind as cloud in lake,
His daughter's crime, distinct and visible,
   Before him stood.   He turned to her and spake :
"Thou hear'st the charge.   How makest thou reply?"
And she : "The deed is mine !   I wrought it !   I ! "


Then spake King Bove with countenance like night :
   "Of all dread shapes that traverse earth or sea,
Or pierce the soil, or urge through heaven their flight,
   Say, which abhorrest thou most?"   And answered
      she :
"The shape of Spirits Accursed that ride the storm. "
And he : " Be thine henceforth that demon form ! "

He spake, and lifted high his Druid Wand.
  T'ward him, perforce, **she** drew; she bowed her
     head;
Down on that head he dropped it; and beyond
  The glooming lake, with bat-like wings outspread
O'er earth's black verge, the shrieking Fury passed:
Thenceforth to **circle** earth while earth shall last.

As when, on autumn eve from hill or cape
  That slants into grey wastes of **western** sea,
The sun long set, some shepherd stares agape
  At cloud that seems through endless space to flee
**On raven** pinions down the moaning **wind,** —
Thus on that **Fury stared they,** well-nigh blind.

**Then spake** the **king with hoary** head that **shook,** —
  " I loved thy babes; now, therefore, **let** us **go**
Northward, and on their blameless beauty **look,**
  **Though** changed, and hear their songs; for this I
     know
By Druid art, they sing **the** whole night long,
And **heaven and earth** are solaced by **their song.**"

**Northward ere** dawn they **rode** with a great host;
  And loosed their steeds by Darvra's mirror clear,
What time purpureal evening, **like** a ghost,
  Stepped from the blue glen **on** the glimmering
     mere;
And camped where stood the ruminating herds
**With** heads forth **leaning** t'ward those human birds.

And ever o'er the wave those swans would come
    To hear man's voice and tell their tale to each,
Swift as the wind and whiter than the foam ;
    Yet never mounted they the bowery beach,
And still swerved backward from the beckoning hand,
Revering thus their stepmother's command.


And ever, when the sacred night descended,
    While with those ripples on the sandy bars
The sighing woods and winds low murmurs blended,
    Their music fell upon them from the stars,
And they gave utterance to that gift divine
In silver song or anthem crystalline.


Who heard that strain no more his woes lamented ;
    The exiled chief forgat his place of pride ;
The prince, ill-crowned, his ruthless deed repented ;
    The childless mother and the widowed bride,
Amid their locks, tear-wet and loosely straying,
Felt once again remembered touches playing.


The words of that high music no one knew ;
    Yet all men felt there lived a meaning there,
Immortal, marvellous, searching, strengthening, true,
    The pledge of some great future, strange and fair,
When sin shall lose her might, and cleansing woe
Shall on the Just some starry crown bestow.

Lulled by that strain, the prophet king let drop
   In death his Druid-Staff by Darvra's side ;
And there, in later years, with happy hope
   King Lir, that mystic requiem listening, died ;
And there those blissful sufferers bore their wrong
All day in weeping and all night in song.


Not once, 'tis whispered in that ancient story,
   They raised their voice God's justice to arraign ;
All patient suffering is expiatory ;
   Their doom was linked with hope of Erin's gain ;
And, like the Holy Elders famed of old,
Those babes on that high promise kept their hold.


And they saw great towers built, and saw them fall ;
   And saw the little seedling tempest-sown ;
And generations under torch and pall
   Borne forth to narrow graves ere long grass-grown ;
And all these things to them were as a dream,
Or shade that sleeps on some fast-hurrying stream.


More numerous daily flocked to that still shore
   Peace-loving spirits ; yea, the Gaelic clans
And tribes Dedannan, foemen there no more,
   From the same fountains brimmed their flowing
      cans,
And washed their kirtles in the same pure rills,
And brought their corn-sheaves to the self-same mills.

Thus, though elsewhere the sons of Erin strove
　　From Aileach's coast and Uladh's marble cliffs
To where by banks of Lee, and Beara's cove,
　　The fishers spread their nets and launched their
　　　　skiffs,
Round Darvra's shores remained inviolate peace ;
There, too, the flocks and fields had best increase.


In that long strife the Gael the victory won ;
　　Tuatha's race, Dedannan, disappeared ;
Yet still the conqueror whispered, sire to son :
　　" Their progeny survives, half scorned, half feared, —
The Fairy Host ; and mansions bright they hold
On moonlight hills, and under waters cold.


" To snare the Gael, perpetual spells they weave ;
　　O'er the wet waste they bid the meteor glide ;
They raise illusive cliffs at morn and eve
　　On wintry coasts ; sea-mantled rocks they hide ;
And shipwrecked sailors eye them o'er the waves,
Dark shapes pygmean couchant in sea-caves.


" Some say that, 'mid the mountains' sunless walls,
　　They throng beneath their stony firmament,
An iron-handed race.    At intervals
　　Through chasm stream-cloven, and through rocky
　　　　rent,
The shepherd hears their multitudinous hum,
As of far hosts approaching, swift yet dumb.

" In those dread vaults, Magian and Alchemist,
    Supreme in every craft of brain and hand,
The mountains' mineral veins they beat and twist ;
    And on red anvils forge them spear and brand
For some predestined battle.   Yea, men say
The island shall be theirs that last great day ! "


## CANTO II

### THE PENANCE OF THE INNOCENTS

WHAT time, forth sliding from the Eternal Gates,
    The centuries three on earth had lived and died,
Thus spake Finola to her snowy mates :
    " No more in this soft haven may we bide.
The second Woe succeeds ; that heavier toil
On Alba's waves, the black sea-strait of Moyle."

Then wept to her in turn the younger three :
    " Alas, the sharp rocks and the salt sea-foam !
Thou, therefore, make the lay, ere yet we flee
    From this our exile's cradle, sweet as home ! "
And thus Finola sang, while, far and near,
The men of Erin wept that strain to hear :

" Farewell, Lough Darvra, with thine isles of bloom !
    Farewell, familiar tribes that grace her shore !
The penance deepens on us, and the doom.
    Farewell !   The voice of man we list no more,
Till he, the Tailkenn, comes to sound the knell
Of darkness, and rings out his gladsome bell."

Thus singing, 'mid their dirge the sentenced soared
   Heaven-high ; then, hanging mute on plumes out-
      spread,
With downcast eye long time that lake explored ;
   And, lastly, with a great cry northward sped.
Then was it Erin's sons, listening that cry,
Decreed : "The man who slays a swan, shall die."


Three days against the northern blast on-flying,
   To Fate obedient and the Will Divine,
They reached, what time the crimson eve was lying
   On Alba's isles and ocean's utmost line,
That huge sea-strait, whose racing eddies boil
'Twixt Erin and the cloud-girt headland, Moyle.


There anguish fell on them ; they heard the booming
   Of league-long breakers white ; and gazed on waves
Wreck-strewn, themselves entombed, and all-en-
      tombing,
   Rolling to labyrinths dim of red-roofed caves ;
And streaming waters broad, as with one will,
In cataracts from grey shelves descending still.


There, day by day, the sun more early set ;
   And through the hollows of the high-ridged sea,
Which foamed around their rocky cabinet,
   The whirlwinds beat them more remorselessly ;
And winter followed soon ; and, ofttimes, storms
Shrouded for weeks the mountains' frowning forms.

In time all ocean omens they had learned ;
   And once, as o'er the darkening deep they roved,
Finola, who the advancing woe discerned,
   Addressed them : " Little brothers, well beloved,
Though many a storm hath tried us, yet the worst
Comes up this night ; now, therefore, ere it burst,

" Devise we swiftly, if, through God's high Will,
   Billow or blast divides us each from each,
Some refuge-house wherein, when winds are still,
   To meet once more — low rock or sandy beach ; "
And answer thus they made : " One spot alone
This night can yield us refuge, Carickrone."

They spake, and sudden thunder shook the world,
   And blackness wrapped the seas, and lightnings
      rent ;
And, each from each, abroad those swans were hurled
   By solid water-scud.   Outworn and spent,
At last, that direful tempest over-blown,
Finola scaled their trysting-rock — alone.

But when she found no gentle brother near,
   And heard the great storm roaring far away,
Anguish of anguish pierced her heart, and fear,
   And thus she made her moan and sang her lay :
" Death-cold they lie along the far sea-tide :
Would that as cold I drifted at their side ! "

Thus as she sang, behold, the sun uprose,
  And smote a swan that on a wave's smooth crest
Exhausted lay, like one by pitiless foes
  Trampled, and looking but to death for rest ;
He also clomb that rock, though weak and worn,
With bleeding feet, and pinions tempest-torn.


Aodh was he !   He couched him by her side ;
  Straight, her right wing Finola o'er him spread.
Ere long, beneath the rock, Fiacre she spied,
  Wounded yet more ; yet soon he hid his head
'Neath her left wing, her nestling's wonted place,
And slept content in that beloved embrace.


But still Finola mused with many a tear, —
  " Alas for us, of little Conn bereft ! "
Then Conn came floating by, full blithe of cheer,
  For he, secure within a craggy cleft,
Had slept all night ; and now once more his nest
He made beneath his snowy sister's breast.


And, as they slept, she sang : " Among the flowers
  Of old we played, where princes quaffed their wine :
But now for flowery fields sea-floods are ours ;
  And now our wine-cup is the bitter brine.
Yet, brothers, fear no ill ; for God will send
At last his Tailkenn, and our woes find end."

And God, Who of least things has tenderest thought,
  Looked down on them benignly from on high,
And bade that bitter brine to enter not
  Their scars, unhealed as yet, lest they should die ;
And nearer sent their choicest food full oft,
And clothed their wings with plumage fine and soft.


And ever, as the spring advanced, the sea
  Put on a kindlier aspect.   Cliffs, deep-scarred,
To milder airs gave welcome festively
  Upon their iron breasts and foreheads hard,
And, while about their feet the ripples played,
Cast o'er the glaring deep a friendlier shade.


And when at last the full midsummer panted
  Upon the austere main and high-peaked isles
And hills that, like some elfin land enchanted,
  Now charmed, now mocked the eye with phantom
      smiles, —
More far round Alba's shores the swans made way
To Islay's beach and cloud-loved Colonsay.


The growths, beside their native lake oft noted,
  In that sublimer clime no more they missed ;
Jewels, not flowers, they found where'er they floated,
  Emerald and sapphire, opal, amethyst,
Far-kenned through watery depths or magic air,
Or trails of broken rainbows, here and there.

II

Round Erin's northern coasts they drifted on
   From Rathlin isle to Fanad's beetling crest,
And where, in frowning sunset steeped, forth shone
   The " Bloody Foreland " gazing t'ward the west ;
Yet still with duteous hearts to Moyle returned —
To love their place of penance they had learned.


One time it chanced that, onward as they drifted,
   Where Banna's current joins that stormy sea,
A princely company, with banners lifted,
   Rode past on snow-white steeds and sang for glee ;
At once they knew those horsemen, form and face,
Their native stock, Tuatha's ancient race !


T'ward them they sped ; their sorrows they recounted ;
   The warriors could not aid them, and rode by.
Then higher than of old their anguish mounted ;
   And farther rang through heaven their piteous cry ;
And when it ceased, this lay Finola sang,
While all the echoing rocks and caverns rang :


" Whilom in purple clad we sat elate ;
   The warriors watched us at their nut-brown mead ;
But now we roam the waters desolate,
   Or breast the languid beds of waving weed ;
Our food was then fine bread ; our drink was wine ;
This day on sea-plants sour we peak and pine.

" Whilom our four small cots of pearl and gold
    Lay, side by side, before our father's bed,
And silken foldings kept us from the cold ;
    But now on restless waves our couch is spread ;
And now our bed-clothes are the white sea-foam ;
And now, by night, the sea-rock is our home."


Not less from them such sorrows swiftly passed,
    Since evermore one thought their bosoms filled —
That father's home.   That haunt, in memory glassed,
    Childhood perpetual o'er their lives distilled ;
And, coast what shore they might, green vale and
        plain
Bred whiter flocks, men said, more golden grain.


The years ran on ; the centuries three went by.
    Finola sang : " The second Woe is ended !"
Obedient then, once more they soared on high ;
    Next morn, on Erin's western coast descended,
While sunrise flashed from misty isles far seen,
Now gold, now flecked with streaks of luminous green.


And there for many a winter they abode,
    Harbouring in precincts of the setting sun ;
And mourned by day, yet sang at night their ode,
    As though in praise of some great victory won,
Some conqueror more than man, some heavenly crown
Slowly o'er all creation settling down.

There once — what time a great sun in decline
   Had changed to gold the green back of a wave
That showered a pasture fair with diamond brine,
   Then sank, anon uprising from its grave
Went shouldering onward, higher and more high,
And hid far lands, and half eclipsed the sky —


There once a shepherd, Aibhric, high of race,
   Marked them far off, and, marking them, so loved
That to the ocean's verge he rushed apace,
   With hands outspread.  Shoreward the creatures
      moved ;
And, when he heard them speak with human tongue,
That love he felt grew tenderer and more strong.


Day after day, they told that youth their tale ;
   Wide-eyed he stood, and inly drank their words ;
And, later, harping still in wood and vale,
   He fitted oft their sorrow to his chords ;
And thus to him in part men owe the lore
Of all those patient sufferers bare of yore.


For bard he was ; and still the bard-like nature
   Hath reverence, as for virtue, so for woe ;
And ever finds, in trials of the creature,
   The great Creator's purpose, here below,
To lift by lowering, and through anguish strange
To fit for thrones exempt from chance or change.

There first the Four had met that sympathy
   Yearned for so long ; and yet, that treasure found,
So much the more, ere long, calamity
   Tasked them, thus strengthened ; tasked, and closed
      them round ;
And higher yet fierce winds and watery shocks
Dashed them thenceforth upon the pitiless rocks.


At last from heaven's dark vault a night there fell,
   The direst they had known.   The high-heaped seas,
Vanquished by frost, beneath her iron spell
   Abased their haughty crests by slow degrees.
The swans were frozen upon that ice-plain frore ;
Yet still Finola sang, as oft before :


" Beneath my right wing, Aodh, make thy rest !
   Beneath my left, Fiacre !   My little Conn,
Find thou a warmer shelter 'neath my breast,
   As thou art wont ; thou art my little son !
Thou, God, that all things mad'st, and lovest all,
Subdue things great !   Protect the weak, the small ! "


But evermore the younger three made moan ;
   And still their moans more loud and louder grew ;
And still Finola o'er that sea of stone
   For their sake fragments of wild wailings threw ;
And ever as she sang, the on-driving snow
Choked the sweet strain ; yet still she warbled low.

Then, louder when she heard those others grieve,
    And found that song might now no more avail,
She said : " Believe, O brothers young, believe
    In that great God, whose help can never fail !
Have faith in God, since God can ne'er deceive ! "
And, lo ! those weepers answered, — " We believe ! "


So thus those babes, in God's predestined hour,
    Through help of Him, the Lord of Life and Death,
Inly fulfilled with light and prophet power,
    Believed, and perfect made their Act of Faith ;
And thenceforth all things, both in shade and shine,
To them came softly and with touch benign.


First, from the southern stars there came a breeze,
    On-wafting happy mist of moonlit rain ;
And, when the sun ascended o'er the seas,
    The ice was vanquished ; and the watery plain,
And every cloud, with rapture thrilled and stirred ;
And, lo ! at noon the cuckoo's voice was heard !


And since with that rough ice their feet were sore,
    God for their sake a breeze from Eden sent,
That gently raised them from the ocean's floor,
    And in its bosom, as an ambient tent,
Held them suspense ; and, with a dew of balm,
God, while they slept, made air and ocean calm.

Likewise a beam auroral forth he sped,
   That flushed that tent aerial, like a rose,
Each morn, and roseate odours o'er it shed
   The long day through. And still, at evening's
      close,
They dreamed of those rich bowers and alleys green,
Wherein with Lir their childish sports had been.


And thrice they dreamed that, in the morning grey,
   They gathered there red roses drenched with dew;
But, lo ! a serpent 'neath the roses lay;
   Then came the Tailkenn, and that serpent slew;
And round the Tailkenn's tonsured head was light
That made the morning more than noonday bright.


Thus wrapt, thus kindled, in sublimer mood
   Heaven-high they soared, and flung abroad their
      strain,
O'er-sailing huge Croagh-Patrick swathed in wood,
   Or Acaill, warder of the western main,
Or Arran Isle, that time heroic haunt,
Since Enda's day Religion's saintlier vaunt.


And many a time they floated farther south,
   Where milder airs endear sea-margins bleak,
To that dim Head far seen o'er Shenan's mouth,
   Or Smerwick's ill-famed cliff and winding creek,
Or where on Brandon sleeps Milesius' son,
With all his shipwrecked warriors round him — Donn.

The centuries passed : her loud, exultant lay
    Finola sang, their time of penance done,
And ended : " Lo, to us it seems a day ;
    Not less the dread nine hundred years are run !
Now, brothers, homeward be our flight ! "    And they
Chanted triumphant : " Home, to Finnaha ! "


Up from the sea they rose, in widening gyre,
    And hung suspended 'mid the ethereal blue,
And saw, far flashing in the sunset's fire,
    A  wood-girt  lake  whose  splendour  well  they
        knew ;
And flew all night ; and reached at dawn its shore —
Ah, then rang out that wail ne'er heard before !


There, where the towers of Lir of old had stood,
    Lay now the stony heap and rain-washed rath ;
And through the ruin-mantling alder-wood
    The forest beast had stamped in mire his path ;
And desolate were their mother's happy bowers,
So fair of old with fountains and with flowers !


More closely drew the orphans each to each.
    'Twas then Finola raised her dirge on high,
As nearer yet they drifted to the beach
    In hope one fragment of past days to spy :
" Upon our father's house hath fallen a change ;
And, as a dead man's face, this place is strange !

" No more the hound and horse ; no more the horn !
. No more the warriors winding down the glen !
Behold, the place of pleasaunce is forlorn,
    And emptied of fair women and brave men ;
The wine-cup now is dry ; the music fled —
Now know we that our father, Lir, is dead ! "


She sang, and ceased, though long the feathered
        throat
    Panted with passion of the unuttered song.
At last she spake, with voice that seemed remote,
    Like echoed voice of one the tombs among:
" Depart we hence !   Better the exile's pain ! "
And they: " Return we to rough waves again ! "


Yet still along that silver mere they lingered,
    Oaring their weeping way by lawn and cape,
Till evening, purple-stoled and dewy-fingered,
    O'er heaven's sweet face had woven its veil of
        crape ;
And tenderer came from darkening wood and wild
The voice far off of woman or of child.


And when, far travelling through the fields of ether,
    The stars successive filled their thrones of light,
Still to that heaven the glimmering lake beneath her
    Gave meet response, with music answering light;
For still, wherever sailed that mystic four,       .
With minstrelsy divine that lake ran o'er.

But when the rising sun made visible
  The night-mist hovering long o'er banks of reed,
They cast their broad wings on a gathering swell
  Of wind that, late from eastern sea-caves freed,
Waved all the island's oakwoods t'ward the West;
And seaward swooped at eve, and there found
    rest.


And since they knew their penance now was over,
  Penance that tasks true hearts to purify,
Happier were they than e'er was mortal lover,
  Happy as Spirits cleansed that, near the sky,
Feel, 'mid that shadowy realm expiatory,
Warm on their lids, the unseen, yet nearing, glory.


Thenceforth they roamed no more, at Inisglaire
  Their change awaiting.   In its blissful prime
That island was, men say, as Eden fair, —
  The swan-soft nursling of a changeful clime,
With amaranth-lighted glades, and tremulous sheen
Of trees full-flowered on earth no longer seen.


Not then the waves with that still site contended;
  On its warm sandhills pansies always bloomed;
And ever with the inspiring sea-wind blended
  The breath of gardens violet-perfumed;
And daisies whitened lawn and dell, and spread
At sunset o'er green hills their under-red,

"Faint as that blush which lights some matron's cheek,
   Tenderly pleased by gentle praise deserved ;
That island's winding coast, from creek to creek,
     Like curves of shells, with dream-like beauty
       swerved ;
And midmost spread a lake, from mortal eyes
Vanished this day, like man's lost paradise.


Around that lake, with oldest oakwoods shaded,
   Were all things that to eye are witching most,
Green slopes dew-drenched, and gray rocks ivy-
     braided ;
   Yet speechless was the region as a ghost ;
No whisper shook those woods ; no tendril stirred ;
Nor e'er within the cave was ripple heard.


A home for Spirits, not home for man, it seemed ;
   Or Limbo meet for body-waiting Souls —
Of such in Pagan times the poets dreamed :
   That stillness, which invests the unmoving poles,
Above it brooded.   In its circuit wide
A second Darvra lived — but glorified.


Upon its breast perpetual light there lay,
   Undazzling beam, and uncreated light ;
For lake and wood the sunshine drank all day,
   And breathed it softly forth to cheer the night, —
A silver twilight, pure from cloud or taint,
Like aureole round the forehead of a saint.

There  dwelt  those  swans ;  there  louder  anthems
    chanted ;
  There first they sang by day rapt song and hymn,
Till all those birds the western coasts that haunted
    Came flying far o'er ocean's purple rim,
Scorning thenceforth wild cliff and beds of foam ;
And made, then first, that sacred isle their home.


So passed three years.   When dawned the third May
    morn,
  The Four, while slowly rose the kindling mist
Showing the first white on the earliest thorn,
    Heard music o'er the waters.   List — O list !
'Twas sweet as theirs — more sweet — yet terrible,
At first ; and sudden trembling on them fell.


A second time it sounded.   Terror died,
    And rapture came instead, and mystic mirth,
They knew not whence ; and thus Finola cried :
    " Brothers ! the Tailkenn treads our Erin's earth ! "
And as the lifted mist gave view more large,
They saw a blue bay with a fair green marge.


On that green marge there rose an Altar-stone ;
    Before it, robed in white, with tonsured head,
Stood up the kingly Tailkenn all alone ;
    Not far behind, in reverence, not in dread,
With low bent brows a princely senate knelt,
Girding that altar as with golden belt.

Marvelling, as on they sailed, that rite they saw ;
   But, when a third time pealed that Tailkenn's bell,
They, too, their halleluias, though with awe,
   Blended with his.   The Ill Spirits heard their knell,
And, shrieking, fled to penal dungeons drear ;
And straight, since now those blissful Four drew near,


.Saint Patrick stretched above the wave his hand,
   And thus he spake — and wind and wave were
      stilled —
" Children of Lir, re-tread your native land,
   For now your long sea-penance is fulfilled ! "
Then, lo ! Finola raised the funeral cry :
" We tread our native land that we may die ! "


And thus she made the lay, and thus she sang :
   " Baptize us, priest, while living yet we be ! "
And louder soon her dirge-like anthem rang :
   " Lo, thus the Children's burial I decree ;
Make fair our grave where land and ocean meet,
And t'ward thy holy Altar place our feet.


" Upon my left, Fiacre ; upon my right
   Let Aodh sleep ; for such their place of rest,
Secured to each by usage day and night ;
   And lay my little Conn upon my breast ;
Then on a low sand pillow raise my head,
That I may see his face though I be dead."

She spake ; and on the sands they stept — the Four —
　　Then, lo ! from heaven there came a miracle.
Soon as they left the wave, and trod the shore,
　　The weight of bygone centuries on them fell ;
To human forms they changed, yet human none ; —
Dread, shapeless weights of wrinkles and of bone.


A moment, prone the wildered creatures lay ;
　　Then, slowly, up that breadth of tawny sand,
Like wounded beast that can but crawl, made way
　　With knee convulsed, and closed and clutching
　　　　hand, —
Nine-centuried forms, still breathing mortal breath,
Though shrouded in the cerements pale of death.


That concourse on them gazed with many a tear ;
　　Yet no man uttered speech or motion made,
Till now the Four had reached that altar-bier,
　　Their ghastly pilgrimage's goal, and laid
Before its base their bodies, one by one,
And faces glistening in the rising sun.


There lying, loud they raised the self-same cry,
　　As Patrick o'er them signed the conquering Sign, —
" Baptize us, holy Tailkenn, for we die ! "
　　The saint baptized them in the name Divine,
And, swift as thought, their happy spirits at last
To God's high feast and singing angels passed.

Now hear the latest wonder.   While, low-bowed,
  That concourse gazed upon the reverend dead,
Behold, like changeful shapes in evening cloud,
  Vanished those time-worn bodies ; and, instead,
Inwoven lay four children, white and young,
With silver-lidded eyes and lashes long.


Finola lay, once more an eight years' child ;
  Upon her right hand Aodh took his rest,
Upon her left Fiacre ; — in death he smiled ;
  Her little Conn was cradled on her breast ;
And all their saintly raiment shone as bright
As sea-foam sparkling on a moonlit night ;


Or, as their snowy night-clothes shone of old,
  When now the night was past, and Lir, their sire,
Upraised them from the warm cot's silken fold,
  And bade them watch the sun's ascending fire,
And watched himself its beam, now here, now there,
Flashed from white foot, blue eyes, or golden hair.


The men who saw that death-bed did not weep,
  But gazed till sunset upon each fair face ;
And then with funeral psalm, and anthems deep,
  Interred them at that sacred altar's base,
And graved their names in Ogham characters
On  one  white  tomb;  and,  close  beneath  them,
    Lir's.

Those Babes were Erin's Holy Innocents,
   And first-fruits of the land to Christ their Lord,
Though born within the unbeliever's tents :
   Figured in them the Gael his God adored, —
That later-coming, holier Gael, who won
Through Faith the birthright, though the younger son.

# MISCELLANEOUS POEMS

FORTH with those missives, Chiron, to the Invader!
Hence, and make speed; they scathe mine eyes like
    fire.
Pompeius, thou hast conquered! What remains?
Vengeance! Man's race has never dreamed of such;
So slow, so sure. Pompeius, I depart.
I might have held these mountains yet four days;
The fifth had seen them thine —
I look beyond the limit of this night.
Four centuries I need; then comes mine hour.

    What saith the Accursed One of the Western World?
I hear even now her trumpet! Thus she saith:
"I have enlarged my borders; iron reaped
Earth's field all golden. Strenuous fight we fought;
I left some sweat-drops on that Carthage shore,
Some blood on Gallic javelins. That is past!
My pleasant days are come. My couch is spread
Beside all waters of the Midland Sea;
By whispers lulled of nations kneeling round;
Illumed by light of balmiest climes; refreshed
By winds from Atlas and the Olympian snows.
Henceforth my foot is in delicious ways;
Bathe it, ye Persian fountains! Syrian vales,
All roses, make me sleepy with perfumes!
Caucasian cliffs, with martial echoes faint,

Flatter light slumbers; charm a Roman dream!
I send you my Pompeius; let him lead
Odin in chains to Rome!"   Odin in chains!
Were Odin chained, or dead, that God he serves
Could raise a thousand Odins. —
Rome's Founder-King, beside his Augur standing,
Noted twelve ravens borne in sequent flight
O'er Alba's crags.   They emblemed centuries twelve,
The term to Rome conceded.   Eight are flown;
Remain but four.   Hail, sacred brood of night!
Henceforth my standards bear the Raven Sign,
The bird that hoarsely haunts the ruined tower;
The bird sagacious of the field of blood
Albeit far off.   Four centuries I need.
Then comes my day.   My race and I are one.

   O Race beloved and holy!   From my youth
Where'er a hungry heart impelled my feet,
Whate'er I found of glorious, have I not
Claimed it for thee, deep-musing?   Ignorant, first,
For thee I wished the golden ingots piled
In Susa and Ecbatana: — ah fool!
At Athens next, treading where Plato trod,
For thee all triumphs of the mind of man,
And Phidian hand inspired!   Ah fool, that hour
Athens lay bound, a slave!   Later to Rome
In secrecy by Mithridates sent
To search the inmost of his hated foe,
For thee I claimed that discipline of Law
Which made her State one camp.   Fool, fool once
      more!

Soon learned I what a heart-pollution lurked
Beneath that mask of Law.   As Persia fell,
By softness sapped, so Rome.   Behold, this day,
Following the Pole Star of my just revenge,
I lead my people forth to clearer fates
Through cloudier fortunes.   They are brave and
     strong;
'Tis but the rose-breath of their vale that rots
Their destiny's bud unblown.   I lead them forth,
A race war-vanquished, not a race of slaves;
Lead them, not Southward to Euphrates' bank,
Not Eastward to the realms of rising suns,
Not West to Rome, and bondage.   Hail, thou North!
Hail, boundless woods, by nameless oceans girt,
And snow-robed mountain islets, founts of fire!
   Four hundred years!   I know that awful North.
I sought it when the one flower of my life
Fell to my foot.   That anguish set me free.
It dashed me on the iron side of life;
I woke, a man.   My people too shall wake;
They shall have icy crags for myrtle banks,
Sharp rocks for couches.   Strength!   I must have
     strength!
Not splenetic sallies of a woman's courage,
But hearts to which self-pity is unknown!
Hard life to them must be as mighty wine
Gladdening the strong; the death on battle-fields
Must seem the natural, honest close of life;
Their fear must be to die without a wound
And miss Life's after-banquet.   Wooden shield

Whole winter nights shall lie their covering sole;
Thereon the boy shall stem the ocean wave;
Thereon the youth shall slide with speed of winds,
Loud-laughing, down the snowy mountain-slope;
To him the Sire shall whisper as he bleeds,
" Remember the revenge!   Thy son must prove
More strong, more hard than thou!"
                      Four hundred years!
Increase is tardy in that icy clime,
For Death is there the awful nurse of Life;
Death rocks the cot.   Why meet we there no wolf
Save those huge-limbed?  Because weak wolf-cubs die.
'Tis thus with man; 'tis thus with all things strong.
Rise higher on thy Northern hills, my Pine!
That Southern Palm shall dwindle.
                   House stone-walled —
Ye shall not have it!   Temples cedar-roofed —
Ye shall not build them!   Where the Temple stands,
The City gathers.   Cities ye shall spurn;
Live in the woods; live singly, winning each,
Hunter or fisher by blue lakes, his prey;
Abhor the gilded shrine; the God Unknown
In such abides not.   On the mountain's top
Great Persia sought Him in her day of strength;
With her ye share the kingly breed of Truths,
The noblest inspirations Man hath known,
Or can know — ay, unless the Lord of all
Should come, Man's Teacher.   Pray as Persia prayed;
And see ye pray for Vengeance!   Leave till then
To Rome her Idol fanes and pilfered Gods.

I see you, O my people, year by year
Strengthened by sufferings; pains that crush the
    weak,
Your helpers.  Men have been that, poison-fed,
Grew poison-proof; on pain and wrong feed ye!
The wild beast rage against you! frost and fire
Rack you in turn!  I'll have no gold among you;
With gold come wants; and wants mean servitude.
Edge, each, his spear with fish-bone or with flint,
Leaning for prop on none.  I want no Nations!
A Race I fashion, playing not at States.
I take the race of Man, the breed that lifts
Alone its brow to heaven; I change that race
From clay to stone, from stone to adamant,
Through slow abrasion, such as leaves sea-shelves
Lustrous at last and smooth.  To *be*, not *have*, —
A man to be; no heritage to clasp
Save that which simple manhood, at its will,
Or conquers or re-conquers, held meanwhile
In trust for Virtue; this alone is greatness.
Remain ye Tribes, not Nations; led by Kings,
Great onward-striding Kings, above the rest
High towering, like the keel-compelling sail
That takes the topmost tempest.  Let them die,
Each for his people!  I will die for mine
Then when my work is finished; not before.
That Bandit King who founded Rome, the Accursed.
Vanished in storm.  My sons shall see me die, —
Die, strong to lead them till my latest breath,
Which shall not be a sigh; shall see and say,  .

"'This Man, far-marching through the mountainous
      world,
No God, but yet God's Prophet of the North,
Gave many crowns to others; for himself,
His people were his crown."
                              Four hundred years!
Ye shall find savage races in your path.
Be ye barbaric, — ay, but savage not;
Hew down the baser, lest they drag you down;
Ye cannot raise them — they fulfil their fates.
Be terrible to foes, be kind to friend.
Be just; be true.    Revere the Household Hearth;
This knowing, that beside it dwells a God.
Revere the Priest, the King, the Bard, the Maid,
The Mother of the heroic race — five strings
Sounding God's Lyre.  Drive out, with lance for goad,
That idiot God by Rome called Terminus,
Who standing sleeps, and holds his reign o'er fools.
The earth is God's, not Man's: that man from Him
Holds it, whose valour earns it.   Time shall come,
It may be, when the warfare shall be past,
The reign triumphant of the brave and just
In peace consolidated.   Time may come
When that long winter of the Northern Land
Shall find its spring.  Where spreads the black morass,
Harvest all gold may glitter; cities rise
Where roamed the elk, — and nations set their thrones;
Nations, not like those empires known till now,
But wise and pure.   Let such their temples build,
And worship Truth, if Truth should e'er to Man

Show her full face.   Let such ordain them laws,
If Justice e'er should mate with laws of men.
Above the mountain summits of Man's hope
There spreads, I know, a land illimitable, —
The table land of Virtue trial-proved,
Whereon, one day, the nations of the world
Shall race like emulous Gods.   A greater God
Served by our sires, a God unknown to Rome,
Above that shining level sits, high-towered;
Millions of Spirits wing His flaming light,
And fiery winds among His tresses play.
When comes that hour which judges Gods and men,
That God shall plague the Gods that filched His name,
And cleanse the Peoples.
                              When ye hear, my sons,
That God uprising in His judgment robes,
And see their dreadful crimson in the West,
Then know ye that the knell of Rome is nigh.
Then stand, and listen!  When His Trumpet sounds,
Forth from your forests and your snows, my sons!
Forth over Ister, Rhenus, Rhodonus,
To Mœsia forth, to Thrace, Illyricum,
Iberia, Gaul; but, most of all, to Rome!
Who leads you thither, leads you not for spoil.
A mission hath he, fair though terrible; —
He makes a pure hand purer, washed in blood.
On, Scourge of God! the Vengeance Hour is come.
   I know that hour, and wait it.   Odin's work
Stands then consummate.   Odin's name, thenceforth,
Goes down to darkness.

                                        Farewell, Ararat!
How many an evening, still and bright as this,
In childhood, youth, or manhood's sorrowing years,
Have I not watched the sunset hanging red
Upon thy hoary brow!   Farewell forever!
A legend haunts thee that the race of Man
In earliest days, a sad and storm-tossed few,
From thy wan heights descended, making way
Into a ruined world.   A storm-tossed race,
But not self-pitying, once again thou seest
Into a world all ruin making way
Whither they know not, yet without a fear.
This hour — lo, there, they pass yon valley's verge! —
In sable weeds that pilgrimage moves on, —
Moves slowly, like thy shadow, Ararat,
That Eastward creeps.   Phantom of glory dead!
Image of greatness that disdains to die!
Move Northward thou!   Whate'er thy fates decreed,
At least that shadow shall be shadow of man,
And not of beast gold-weighted!   On, thou Night,
Cast by my heart!   Thou, too, shall meet thy morn!

## I

### THE GREAT CONTENTION

Not seldom crossed by bodings sad,
  In words though kind yet hard,
Spake Patrick to his guest, Oiseen;
  For Patrick loved the bard,

In whose broad bosom, swathed with beard
  Like cliffs with ivy trailed,
A Christian strove with a Pagan soul,
  And neither quite prevailed.

Silent as shades the shadowing monks
  O'er cloistral courts might glide;
But the War-Bard strode through the church itself
  Like hunter on mountain-side.

The Priest might soften his Compline psalm
  Till it seemed but the night-wind's sigh;
Oiseen, if the stag-hunt swept by at mass,
  Would echo the stag-hound's cry!

And thus one day, while his beads he told,
  Fierce thoughts, a rebel breed,
Burst up from old graves in the warrior's heart,
  And he stormed at priest and creed.

"Woe, woe! for the priestly tribe this hour
  On the Feine Hill have sway!
Glad am I that scarce their shapes I see;
  Half-blind am I this day.

"Woe, woe, thou Palace of Cruachan!
  Thy sceptre is down and thy sword;
The chase goes over thy grassy roof,
  The monk in thy courts is lord!

"Thou man with the mitre and vestments broad,
  And the bearing of grave command,
Rejoice that Diarmid this day is dust!
  Right heavy was his clenched hand!

"Thou man with the bell! I rede thee well:
  Were Diorring living this day,
Thy book he would take, and thy bell would break
  On the base of yon pillar grey!

"Thou man with miraculous crosier-staff,
  Though puissant thou art, and tall,
Were Goll but here, he would dash thy gear
  In twain on thy convent wall!

"Were Conan living, the bald-head shrill,
  With the scourge of his scoff and gibe
He would break thy neck, and thy convent wreck,
  And lash from the land thy tribe!

"But one of our chiefs had spared thy head —
  My Oscar, my son, my child!
He was storm in the foray and fire in the fight,
  But in peace he was maiden-mild."


Then Patrick answered: "Old man, old man,
  That Pagan realm lies low.
Our home is thine!   Forget thy chiefs,
  And thy deeds gone by forego!


"High feast thou hast on the festal days,
  And cakes on the days of fast — "
"Thou liest, thou priest, for in wrath and scorn
  Thy cakes to the dogs I cast!"


"Old man, thou hearest our Christian hymns;
  Such strains thou hadst never heard — "
"Thou liest, thou priest! for in Letter Lee wood
  I have listened its famed blackbird!


"I have heard the music of meeting swords,
  And the grating of barks on the strand,
And the shout from the breasts of the men of help
  That leaped from the decks to land!


"Twelve hounds had my sire, with throats like bells,
  Loud echoed on lake and bay;
By this hand, they lacked but the baptism rite
  To chaunt with thy monks this day!"

Oiseen's white head on his breast dropt down,
  Till his hair and his beard, made one,
Shone out like the spine of a frosty hill
  Far seen in the wintry sun.


"One question, Patrick! I ask of thee,
  Thou king of the saved and shriven:
My sire, and his chiefs, have they their place
  In thy City, star-built, of heaven?"


"Oiseen, old chief of the harp and sword,
  That questionest of the soul,
That City they tread not who love but war:
  Their realm is a realm of dole."


"By this head, thou liest, thou son of Calphurn!
  In heaven I would scorn to bide
If my father and Oscar were exiled men,
  And no friend at my side."


"That City, old man, is the City of Peace;
  Loud anthems, not widows' wail."
"It is not in bellowings chiefs take joy,
  But in songs of the wars of Fail!


"Are the men in the streets like Baoignè's chiefs?
  Great-hearted like us are they?
Do they stretch to the poor the ungrudging hand,
  Or turn they their heads away?

"Thou man with the chaunt, and thou man with the
    creed,
  This thing I demand of thee:
My dog, may he pass through the gates of heaven?
  May my wolf-hound enter free?"

"Old man, not the buzzing gnat may pass,
  Nor sunbeam look in unbidden;
The King, there sceptred, knows all, sees all;
  From Him there is nothing hidden."

"It never was thus with Fionn, our king!
  In largess our Fionn delighted;
The hosts of the earth came in and went forth
  Unquestioned, and uninvited!"

"Thy words are the words of madness, old man,
  Thy chieftains had rule one day;
Yet a moment of heaven is three times worth
  The warriors of Eire for aye!"

Then Oiseen uplifted his old white head:
  Like lightning from hoary skies
A flash went forth 'neath the shaggy roofs
  Low-bent o'er his sightless eyes:

"Though my life sinks down, and I sit in the dust,
  Blind warrior and grey-haired man,
Mine were they of old, thou priest over bold,
  Those chiefs of Baoignè's clan!"

And he cried, while a spasm his huge frame shook,
  "Dim shadows, like men, before me,
My father was Fionn, and Oscar my son,
  Though to-day ye stand vaunting it o'er me!"

Thus raged Oiseen, 'mid the fold of Christ
  Still roaming old deserts wide
In the storm of thought, like a lion old;
  Though lamblike at last he died.

## II

### OISEEN'S YOUTH

"Old man, for once thy chiefs forget — "
  (Thus oft the Saint his rage beguiled)
"Sing us thine own glad youth, while yet
  A stripling, or a child."

"O Patrick, glad that time and dear!
  It wrought no greatness, gained no gain;
Not less those things thou long'st to hear
  Thou shalt not seek in vain.

"My mother was a princess, turned
  By magic to a milk-white doe:—
Such tale, a wondering child, I learned.
  True was it?  Who can know?

"I know but this, that yet a boy,
    I raced beside her like the wind;
We heard the hunter's horn with joy,
    And left the pack behind.

"A strength was mine that knew no bound,
    A witless strength that nothing planned;
When came the hour, the deed I found
    Unsought for in my hand.

"Forth from a cave I stept at Beigh;
    O'er mountain cliffs the loose clouds rushed;
With them I raced, and reached ere they
    The loud seas sandhill-hushed.

"By Brandon's Head an eagle brown
    O'erhung our wave-borne coracle;
I hurled at him my lance, and down
    Like falling stars he fell.

"On that green shore of Ardrakese
    I made an untamed horse my slave,
And forced him far o'er heaving seas,
    And reinless rode the wave.

"Methinks my brow I might have laid
    Against a bull's, and there and then
Have pushed him backward up the glade,
    And down the rocky glen!

K

"So ran my youth through dark and bright
    In deeds half jest.  Their time is gone.
The glorious works of thoughtful might
    For Oscar were, and Fionn!

"Where met the hosts, in mirth I fought;
    My war-fields still with revel rang;
My sword with such a God was fraught
    That while it smote it sang!

" My spear, unbidden, to my hand
    Leaped, hawk-wise, for the battle's sake;
Forth launched, it flashed along the land
    With music in its wake.

"I bore a shield, so charged and stored
    With rage and yearnings for the fight,
When foes drew near, it shook, and roared
    Like breakers in the night;

"But when at last the iron feast
    Of war its hungry heart had stilled,
It murmured like a whispering priest
    Or frothing pail new-filled!"

"Say, knew'st thou never fear or awe?"
    Thus Patrick; and the Bard replied,
"Yea, once: for once a man I saw
    Who — not in battle — died!

"I sang the things I loved: the fight;
　The chance inspired that all decides;
That pause of death, when Fate and Flight
　Drag back the battle tides;

"The swords that blent their lightnings blue;
　The midnight march; the city's sack;
The advancing ridge of spears that threw
　The levelled sunrise back.

"And yet my harp could still the storm,
　Redeem the babe from magic blight,
Restore to human heart and form
　The unhappy spell-bound knight.

"And some could hear a sobbing hind
　Among my chords; and some would swear
They heard that kiss of branch and wind
　That lulled the wild-deer's lair!

"I sang not lusts; where base men thronged
　I sat not, neither harped for gold;
My song no gracious foeman wronged,
　No woman's secret told.

"I sang not hate; with healing breath
　Gladness of heaven my harp-strings flung
On bosoms true, but shamed to death
　False heart, and ruthless tongue.

"I sang not lies; amid the flocks
    I sang when sunset flushed the spray,
Or when the white moon scaled the rocks
    And glared upon the bay.

"My stately music I rehearsed
    On shadowing cliffs, when, far below,
In rolled the moon-necked wave, and burst,
    And changed black shores to snow.

"But now I tread a darker brink;
    Far down, unfriendlier waters moan;
And, now, of vanished times I think;
    Now, of that bourn unknown.

"I strike my harp; I make good cheer;
    Yet scarce myself can catch its sound;
I see but phantoms bending near
    When feasters press around.

"Say, Patrick of the mystic lore,
    Shall I, when this old head lies low,
My Oscar see, and Fionn, once more,
    And race beside that Doe?"

# AENGUS

When Patrick now o'er Ulster's forest bound,
And Connact, echoing to the western wave,
And Leinster, fair with hill-suspended woods,
Had raised the cross, and where the deep night ruled
Splendour had sent of everlasting light,
Sole peace of warring hearts, — to Munster next,
Thomond and Desmond, Heber's portion old,
He turned; and, fired by love that mocks at rest,
Pushed on, through raging storm, the whole night
    long,
Intent to hold the Annunciation Feast
At Cashel of the Kings. The royal keep
High-seated on its Rock, as morning broke,
Faced them at last; and at the self-same hour
Aengus, in his father's absence lord,
Rising from happy sleep and heaven-sent dreams,
Went forth on duteous tasks. With sudden start
The prince stept back; for, o'er the fortress court,
Like grove storm-levelled lay the idols huge,
False Gods and foul, that long had awed the land,
Prone, without hand of man. O'er-awed, he gazed.
Then on the air there rang a sound of hymns,
And by the eastern gate Saint Patrick stood,
The brethren round him. On their shaggy garb
Auroral mist, struck by the rising sun,
Glittered, that diamond-panoplied they seemed,

And as a heavenly vision.   At that sight
The youth, descending with a wondering joy,
Welcomed his guests; and, ere an hour, the streets,
Far down, shone out like flowering meads in spring,—
So thronged the folk in holiday attire
To see the man far-famed.   "Who spurns our Gods?"
Once they had cried in wrath; but, year by year,
Tidings of some deliverance great and strange,
Some life more noble, some sublimer hope,
Some regal race enthroned beyond the grave,
Had reached them from afar.   The best believed,
Great hearts for whom nor earthly love sufficed,
Nor earthly fame.   The meaner scoffed; yet all
Desired the man.   Delay had edged their thirst.

Then Patrick, standing up among them, spake,
And God was with him.   Not as when loose tongue
Babbles vain rumour, or the Sophist spins
Thought's air-hung cobwebs gay with Fancy's dews,
Spake he, but words of might, as when a man
Bears witness to the things which he has seen,
And tells of that he knows; and as the harp
Attested is by rapture of the ear,
And sunlight by consenting of the eye
That, seeing, knows it sees, and neither craves
Inferior demonstration, — so his words,
Self-proved, went forth and conquered; for man's
     mind,
Created in His image who is Truth,
Challenged by truth, with recognising voice

Cries out, — "Flesh of my flesh, bone of my bone,"
And cleaves thereto.   In all that listening host
One vast, dilating heart yearned to its God.
Then burst the bond of years.   No pause of doubt
They knew.   God laid on them the robe of Truth
Sun-like; down fell the many-coloured weed
Of error; and, reclothed ere yet unclothed,
They walked a new-born earth.   The blinded Past
Fled, vanquished.   Glorious more than strange it
    seemed,
That He who fashioned man should come to man,
And raise by ruling.   They, His trumpet heard,
In glory spurned demons misdeemed for Gods.
Their great chief had returned; the clan enthralled
Trod down the usurping foe.
                    Then rose the cry, —
"Join us to Christ!"   His strong eyes on them set,
Patrick replied, — "Know ye what thing ye seek,
Ye that would fain be house-mates with my King?
Ye seek His cross!"   He paused, then added slow:
"If ye be liegeful, sirs, decree the day,
His baptism shall be yours."
                  That eve, while shone
The sunset on the green-touched woods, that, grazed
By onward flight of unalighting spring,
Caught warmth yet scarcely flamed, Aengus stood
With Patrick in a westward-facing tower
Which overlooked far regions, town-besprent
And lit with winding waters.   Thus he spake:
"My Father! what is sovereignty of man?

Say, can I shield yon host from death, from sin,
Taking them up into my breast, like God?
I trow not so!   Mine be the lowliest place,
Following thy King who left his Father's throne
To walk the lowliest!"   Patrick answered thus:
" Best lot thou choosest, son.   If thine that lot
Thou know'st not yet; nor I.   The Lord, thy God,
Will teach us."
                    When the day decreed had dawned,
Loud rang the bull-horn; and on every breeze
Floated the banners, saffron, green, and blue;
While, issuing from the horizon's utmost verge,
The full-voiced People flocked.   So swarmed of old
Some migratory nation, instinct-urged
To fly their native wastes, sad winter's realm;
So thronged on southern slopes when, far below,
Shone out the plains of promise.   Bright they came!
No summer sea could wear a blithesomer sheen,
Though every dancing crest and milky plume
Ran on with rainbows braided.   Minstrel songs
Wafted like winds those onward hosts, or swayed,
Or stayed them; while among them heralds passed,
Lifting white wands of office.   Foremost rode
Ailcel, the younger brother of the prince.
He ruled a milk-white horse.   Fluttered, breeze-borne,
His mantle green, while all his golden hair
Streamed back redundant from the ring of gold
Circling his head uncovered.   Loveliest light
Of innocence and joy was on that face;
Full well the young maids marked it!   Brighter yet

Beamed he, his brother noting. On the verge
Of Cashel's Rock that hour Aengus stood,
By Patrick's side. That concourse nearer now,
He gazed upon it, crying, with clasped hands:
"My Father, fair is sunrise, fair the sea,
The hills, the plains, the wind-stirred wood, the maid!
But what is like a People onward borne
In gladness? When I see that sight, my heart
Opens like palace-gates wide open flung,
That say to all men, 'Enter.'" Then the Saint
Laid on that royal head a hand of might,
And said: "The Will of God decrees thee King!
Son of this People art thou; Sire, one day,
Thou shalt be! Son and Sire in one are King.
Shepherd for God thy flock, thou Shepherd true!"
He spake: that word was ratified in Heaven.

Meantime that multitude innumerable
Had reached the Rock; and, now the winding road
In pomp ascending, faced those fair-wrought gates,
Which, by the warders at the prince's sign
Drawn back, to all gave entrance. In they streamed,
Filling the central courtway. Patrick stood,
High stationed on a prostrate idol's base,
In vestments of the Vigil of that Feast,
The Annunciation, which with annual boon
Whispers, while melting snows dilate those streams
Purer than snows, to universal earth
That Maiden Mother's joy. The Apostle watched
The advancing throng, and gave them welcome thus:

"As though into the great Triumphant Church,
O guests of God, ye flock!   Her place is Heaven.
Sirs! we this day are militant below;
Not less, advance in faith.   Behold your crowns —
Obedience and Endurance."
                                        There and then
The Rite began: his people's Chief and Head,
Beside the font Aengus stood; his face
Sweet as a child's, yet grave as front of eld;
For reverence he had laid his crown aside,
And from the deep hair to the unsandalled feet
Was raimented in white.   With mitred head
And massive book, forward Saint Patrick leaned,
Stayed by the gem-wrought crosier.   Prayer on prayer
Went up to God; while gift on gift from God,
All Angel-like, invisibly to man,
Descended.   Thrice above that princely brow
Patrick the cleansing waters poured, and traced
Three times thereon the Venerable Sign,
Naming the Name Triune.   The Rite complete,
Awestruck that concourse downward gazed.   At last
Lifting their eyes, they marked the prince's face,
That pale it was though bright, anguished and pale,
While from his naked foot a blood-stream gushed
And o'er the pavement welled.   The crosier's point,
Weighted with weight of all that priestly form,
Had pierced it through.   "Why suffer'dst thou so
        long
The pain in silence?"   Patrick spake, heart-grieved.
Smiling, Aengus answered, "O my Sire,

I thought, thus called to follow Him Whose feet
Were pierced with nails, haply the blissful Rite
Bore witness to their sorrows."

                           At that word
The large eyes of the Apostolic man
Grew larger; and within them lived that light
Not fed by moon or sun, a visible flash
Of that invisible lightning which from God
Vibrates ethereal through the world of souls, —
Vivific strength of Saints.   The mitred brow
Uptowered sublime; the strong, yet wrinkled hands,
Ascending, ceased not, till the crosier's head
Glittered above the concourse like a star.
At last, his hands disparting, down he drew
From Heaven the Royal Blessing, speaking thus:
" For this cause may the blessing, Sire of Kings,
Cleave to thy seed for ever!   Spear and sword
Before them fall!   In glory may the race
Of Nafrach's sons, Aengus and Aileel,
Hold sway on Cashel's summit!   Be their Kings
Great-hearted men, potent to rule and guard
Their people; just to judge them; warriors strong;
Sage counsellors; faithful shepherds; men of God;
That so through them the everlasting King
May flood their land with blessing."   Thus he spake.
And round him all that nation said, — "Amen."

    Thus held they feast in Cashel of the Kings
That day, till all that land was clothed with Christ.
And when the parting came from Cashel's steep,
The Apostle thus the People's Blessing sent:

"The Blessing fall upon the pasture broad,
On fruitful mead, and every corn-clad hill,
And woodland rich with flowers that children love!
Unnumbered be the homesteads, and the hearths!
A blessing on the women, and the men,
On youth, and maiden, and the suckling babe!
A blessing on the fruit-bestowing tree,
And foodful river tide!    Be true; be pure;
Not living from below, but from above,
As men that over-top the world.    And raise
Here, on this rock, high place of idols once,
A kingly church to God.    The same shall stand
For aye, or, wrecked, from ruin rise restored,
His witness till He cometh.    Over Eire
The Blessing speed till time shall be no more
From Cashel of the Kings!"

                    The Saint forth fared.
The People bare him through their kingdom broad
With banner and with song; but o'er its bound
The women of that People followed still,
A half day's journey, with lamenting voice;
Then silent stood, lifting their babes on high;
And, crowned with twofold blessing, home returned.

# THE BARD ETHELL

## I

I am Ethell, the son of Conn;
    Here I bide at the foot of the hill;
I am clansman to Brian and servant to none;
    Whom I hated I hate, whom I loved love still.
Blind am I.   On milk I live,
    And meat, God sends it, on each Saint's Day,
Though Donald Mac Art — may he never thrive! —
    Last Shrovetide drove half my kine away.

## II

At the brown hill's base, by the pale blue lake,
    I dwell, and see the things I saw:
The heron flap heavily up from the brake,
    The crow fly homeward with twig or straw,
The wild duck, a silver line in wake,
    Cutting the calm mere to far Bunaw.
And the things that I heard, though deaf, I hear:
From the tower in the island the feastful cheer;
The horn from the wood; the plunge of the stag,
With the loud hounds after him, down from the crag.
Sweet is the chase, but the battle is sweeter;
More healthful, more joyous, for true men meeter!

### III

My hand is weak! it once was strong;
  My heart burns still with its ancient fire;
If any man smites me he does me wrong,
  For I was the Bard of Brian Mac Guire.
If any man slay me — not unaware,
  By no chance blow, nor in wine and revel —
I have stored beforehand a curse in my prayer
  For his kith and kindred: his deed is evil.

### IV

There never was King, and there never will be,
In battle or banquet like Malachi!
The Seers his reign had predicted long;
He honoured the Bards, and gave gold for song.
If rebels arose, he put out their eyes;
  If robbers plundered, or burned the fanes,
He hung them in chaplets, like rosaries,
  That others, beholding, might take more pains.
There was none to women more reverent-minded,
  (For he held his mother, and Mary, dear);
If any man wronged them, that man he blinded,
  Or straight amerced him of hand or ear.
There was none who founded more convents — none.
  In his palace the old and poor were fed;
The orphan walked, and the widow's son,
  Without groom or page to his throne or bed.
In council he mused, with great brows divine,
And eyes like the eyes of the musing kine,

Upholding a Sceptre o'er which, men said,
Seven Spirits of Wisdom, like fire-tongues, played.
He drained ten lakes and he built ten bridges;
　　He bought a gold book for a thousand cows;
He slew ten Princes who brake their pledges;
　　With the bribed and the base he scorned to carouse
He was sweet and awful; through all his reign
God gave great harvests to vale and plain.
From his nurse's milk he was kind and brave;
And when he went down to his well-wept grave,
Through the triumph of penance his soul uprose
To God and the Saints.　Not so his foes!


## V


The King that came after! ah woe, woe, woe!
He doubted his friend and he trusted his foe.
He bought and he sold; his kingdom old
　　He pledged and pawned to avenge a spite;
No Bard or prophet his birth foretold;
　　He was guarded and warded both day and night;
He counselled with fools and had boors at his feast;
He was cruel to Christian and kind to beast;
Men smiled when they talked of him far o'er the
　　　　wave;
Paid were the mourners that wept at his grave!
God plagued for his sake his people sore:—
　　They sinned; for the people should watch and pray
That their prayers, like angels at window and door,
　　May keep from the King the bad thought away!

## VI

The sun has risen: on lip and brow
   He greets me — I feel it — with golden wand.
Ah, bright-faced Norna!   I see thee now;
   Where first I saw thee, I see thee stand!
From the trellis the girl looked down on me;
   Her maidens stood near; it was late in spring:
The grey priests laughed as she cried in glee, —
   "Good Bard, a song in my honour sing!"
I sang her praise in a loud-voiced hymn
To God who had fashioned her, face and limb,
For the praise of the clan and the land's behoof;
So she flung me a flower from the trellis roof.
Ere long I saw her the hill descending —
   O'er the lake the May morning rose moist and slow;
She prayed me, her smile with the sweet voice blend-
      ing,
   To teach her all that a woman should know.
Panting she stood; she was out of breath;
   The wave of her little breast was shaking;
From eyes still childish, and dark as death,
   Came womanhood's dawn through a dew-cloud
      breaking.
Norna was never long time the same;
   By a spirit so strong was her slight form moulded,
The curves swelled out from the flower-like frame,
   In joy; in grief, to a bud she folded;
As she listened, her eyes grew bright and large,
Like springs rain-fed that dilate their marge.

## VII

So I taught her the hymn of Patrick, the Apostle,
  And the marvels of Bridget and Columkille;
Ere long she sang like the lark or the throstle,
  Sang the deeds of the servants of God's high Will.
I told her of Brendan who found afar
Another world 'neath the western star;
Of our three great bishops in Lindisfarne isle;
Of St. Fursey the wondrous, Fiacre without guile;
Of Sedulius, hymn-maker when hymns were rare;
Of Scotus, the subtle, who clove a hair
Into sixty parts, and had marge to spare.
To her brother I spake of Oisin and Fionn,
And they wept at the death of great Oisin's son.
I taught the heart of the boy to revel
  In tales of old greatness that never tire,
And the virgin's, up-springing from earth's low
    level,
  To wed with heaven like the altar fire.
I taught her all that a woman should know;
  And that none might teach her worse lore, I gave
    her
A dagger keen, and I taught her the blow
  That subdues the knave to discreet behaviour.
A sand-stone there on my knee she set,
And sharpened its point — I can see her yet —
I held back her hair, and she sharpened the edge,
While the wind piped low through the reeds and
    sedge.

L

### VIII

She died in the convent on Ina's height.
   I saw her the day that she took the veil:
As slender she stood as the Paschal light,
   As tall and slender and bright and pale!
I saw her; and dropped as dead.   Bereaven
Is earth, when her holy ones leave her for heaven.
Her brother fell in the fight at Beigh.
May they plead for me, both, on my dying day!

### IX

All praise to the man who brought us the Faith!
'Tis a staff by day and our pillow in death!
All praise, I say, to that blessed youth,
   Who heard, in a dream, from Tyrawley's strand,
   That wail, — "Put forth o'er the sea thy hand;
In the dark we die; give us hope and Truth!"
But Patrick built not on Iorras' shore
   That convent where now the Franciscans dwell;
Columba was mighty in prayer and war;
   But the young monk preaches, as loud as his bell,
That love must rule all, and all wrongs be forgiven,
Or else, he is sure, we shall reach not heaven!
This doctrine I count right cruel and hard;
And, when I am laid in the old churchyard,
The habit of Francis I will not wear;
Nor wear I his cord, or his cloth of hair,
In secret.   Men dwindle: till psalm and prayer
Had softened the land, no Dane dwelt there!

### x

I forgive old Cathbar who sank my boat;
  Must I pardon Feargal who slew my son?
Or the pirate, Strongbow, who burned Granote,
  They tell me, and in it nine priests, a nun,
And — worst — Saint Finian's old crosier staff?
At forgiveness like that I spit and laugh!
My chief, in his wine-cups, forgave twelve men;
And of these a dozen rebelled again!
There never was chief more brave than he!
  The night he was born Loch Gur up-burst.
He was bard-loving, gift-making, loud of glee,
  The last to fly, to advance the first.
He was like the top spray upon Uladh's oak,
  He was like the tap-root of Argial's pine;
He was secret and sudden; as lightning his stroke;
  There was none that could fathom his hid design!
He slept not; if any man scorned his alliance
He struck the first blow for a frank defiance
With that look in his face, half night half light,
Like the lake gust-blackened yet ridged with white!
There were comely wonders before he died:
The eagle barked, and the Banshee cried;
The witch-elm wept with a blighted bud;
The spray of the torrent was red with blood;
The chief, returned from the mountain's bound,
Forgat to ask after Bran, his hound.
We knew he would die: three days were o'er; —
He died.  We *waked* him for three days more.

One by one, upon brow and breast,
The whole clan kissed him.    In peace may he rest!


XI

I sang his dirge.    I could sing that time
Four thousand staves of ancestral rhyme.
To-day I can scarcely sing the half;
Of old I was corn and now I am chaff!
My song to-day is a breeze that shakes
   Feebly the down on the cygnet's breast;
'Twas then a billow the beach that rakes,
   Or a storm that buffets the mountain's crest.
Whatever I bit with a venomed song,
   Grew sick, were it beast, or tree, or man;
The wronged one sued me to right his wrong
   With the flail of the Satire and fierce Ode's fan.
I sang to the chieftains; each stock I traced,
Lest lines should grow tangled through fraud or
      haste.
To princes I sang in a loftier tone, —
Of Moran, the Just, who refused a throne;
Of Moran, whose torque would close, and choke
The wry-necked witness that falsely spoke.
I taught them how to win love and hate,
Not love from all; and to shun debate.
To maids in the bower I sang of love;
And of war at the feastings in bawn or grove.

## XII

Great is our Order; but greater far
 Were its pomp and power in the days of old,
When the five Chief Bards in peace or war
 Had thirty bards each in his train enrolled;
When Ollave Fodhla in Tara's hall
 Fed bards and kings; when the boy, king Nial,
Was trained by Torna; when Britain and Gaul
 Sent crowns of laurel to Dallan Forgial.
To-day we can launch the clans into fight;
 That day we could freeze them in mid career!
Whatever man knows, was our realm bright;
 The lore without music no Gael would hear.
Old Cormac, the brave blind king, was bard
Ere fame rose yet of O'Daly and Ward.
The son of Milesius was bard — "Go back,
 My People," he sang; "ye have done a wrong!
Nine waves go back o'er the green sea track;
 Let your foes their castles and coasts make strong.
To the island ye came by stealth and at night;
She is ours, if we win her in all men's sight!"
For that first song's sake let our bards hold fast
To Truth and Justice from first to last!
'Tis over! some think we erred through pride,
Though Columba the vengeance turned aside.
Too strong we were not; too rich we were;
 Give wealth to knaves: — 'tis the true man's snare!

### XIII

But now men lie; they are just no more;
  They forsake the old ways; they quest for new;
They pry and they snuff after strange false lore
  As dogs hunt vermin!   It never was true : —
I have scorned it for twenty years — this babble
That eastward and southward a Saxon rabble
Have won great battles, and rule large lands,
And plight with daughters of ours their hands!
We know the bold Norman o'erset their throne
Long since!   Our lands!   Let them guard their own!

### XIV

How long He leaves me — the great God — here!
  Have I sinned some sin, or has God forgotten?
This year I think is my hundredth year.
  I am like a bad apple, unripe yet rotten!
They shall lift me ere long, they shall lay me — the
        clan —
By the strength of men on mount Cruachan!
God has much to think of!   How much He hath seen,
And how much is gone by that once hath been!
On sandy hillswhere the rabbits burrow
  Are Raths of Kings men name not now;
On mountain tops I have tracked the furrow,
  And found in forests the buried plough.
For one now living the strong land then
Gave kindly food and raiment to ten.

No doubt they waxed proud and their God defied;
   So their harvest He blighted or burned their hoard:
   Or He sent them plague, or He sent the sword;
Or He sent them lightning; and so they died
Like Dathi, the king, on the dark Alp's side.


### XV

Ah me, that man, who is made of dust,
   Should have pride toward God! 'Tis a demon's
      spleen!
I have often feared lest God, the All-just,
   Should bend from heaven and sweep earth clean, --
Should sweep us all into corners and holes,
Like dust of the house-floor, both bodies and souls!
I have often feared He would send some wind
In wrath; and the nation wake up, stone-blind.
In age or in youth we have all wrought ill.
I say not our great king Nial did well,
Although he was Lord of the Pledges Nine,
   When, besides subduing this land of Eire,
He raised in Armorica banner and sign,
   And wasted the British coast with fire.
Perhaps in his mercy the Lord will say, —
"These men! God's help! 'Twas a rough boy-
     play!"
He is certain — that young Franciscan Priest —
God sees great sin where men see least;
Yet this were to give unto God the eye —
Unmeet the thought — of the humming fly!

I trust there are small things He scorns to see,
In the lowly who cry to Him piteously.
   Our hope is Christ.   I have wept full oft
He came not to Eire in Oisin's time;
   Though love, and those new monks, would make men soft
       men soft
If they were not hardened by war and rhyme.
I have done my part; my end draws nigh;
I shall leave old Eire with a smile and sigh;
She will miss not me as I missed my son;
Yet for her, and her praise, were my best deeds
       done.
Man's deeds! man's deeds! they are shades that fleet,
Or ripples like those that break at my feet;
The deeds of my chief and the deeds of my King
Grow hazy, far seen, like the hills in spring.
Nothing is great save the death on the Cross!
   But Pilate and Herod I hate, and know,
   Had Fionn lived then, he had laid them low,
Though the world thereby had sustained great loss.
My blindness and deafness and aching back
With meekness I bear for that suffering's sake;
And the Lent-fast for Mary's sake I love,
And the honour of Him, the Man above!
My songs are all over now: — so best!
They are laid in the heavenly Singer's breast,
Who never sings but a star is born;
May we hear His song in the endless morn!
I give glory to God for our battles won
   By wood or river, on bay or creek;

For Norna — who died; for my father, Conn;
   For feasts, and the chase on the mountains bleak;
I bewail my sins, both unknown and known,
And of those I have injured forgiveness seek;
The men that were wicked to me and mine
(Not quenching a wrong, nor in war nor wine)
I forgive and absolve them all, save three: —
May Christ in His mercy be kind to me!

# SAINT CUTHBERT'S PENTECOST

SAINT CUTHBERT, yet a youth, for many a year
Walked up and down the green Northumbrian vales,
Well loving God and man.  The rockiest glens,
And promontories shadowing loneliest seas,
Where lived the men least cared for, most forlorn,
He sought, and brought to each the words of peace.
Where'er he went, he preached that God, all Love ;
For, as the sun in heaven, so flamed in him
That love which later fired Assisi's Saint.
Yea, rumour ran that every mountain beast
Obeyed his loving call ; that, when all night
He knelt upon the frosty hills in prayer,
The hare would couch her by his naked feet
And warm them with her fur.  To manhood grown,
He dwelt in Lindisfarne ; there, year by year,
Prospering yet more in vigil and in fast ;
And paced its shores by night, and blent his hymns
With din of waves.  Yet ofttimes o'er the strait
He passed, once more in search of suffering men,
Wafting them solace still.  Where'er he went,
Those loved as children first, again he loved
As youth and maid, and in them nursed that Faith
Through which pure youth passes o'er passion's waves,
Like Him Who trod that Galilean sea.
He clasped the grey-grown sinner in his arms,
And won from him repentance long delayed,

Then with him shared the penance he enjoined.
O heart both strong and tender ! offering Mass,
Awe-struck he stood, as though on Calvary's height :
The men who marked him shook.

      Twelve winters passed.
Then mandate fell upon the Saint from God,
Or breathed upon him from the heavenly height,
Or haply from within. It drave him forth,
A hermit into solitudes more stern.
" Farewell," he said, " my brethren and my friends !
No holier life than yours, pure Cœnobites,
Pacing one cloister, sharing one spare meal,
Chanting to God one hymn ! yet I must forth —
Farewell, my friends, farewell !" On him they gazed,
And knew that God had spoken to his soul,
And silent stood, though sorrowing.

      Long, that eve,
The brethren grieved, noting his vacant stall,
Yet thus excused their sadness : " Well for him,
And high his place in heaven ; but woe to those,
Henceforth of services like his amerced !
Here lived he in the world ; here many throng.
To him in time some lesser bishopric
Might well have fallen, behoof of countless souls !
Such dream is past forever !"

      Forth he fared
To Farne, a little rocky islet nigh,
Where man till then had never dared to dwell,
By dreadful rumours scared. In narrow cave,
Worn from the rock, and roughly walled around,

The anchoret made abode, with lonely hands
Raising from one poor strip his daily food,
Barley thin-grown, and coarse.   He saw by day
The clouds on-sailing, and by night the stars ;
And heard the eternal waters.   Thus recluse,
The man lived on in vision still of God
Through contemplation known ; and, as the shades
Each other chase all day o'er steadfast hills,
Even so, athwart that Vision unremoved,
Forever rushed the tumults of this world,
Man's fleeting life, the rise and fall of states,
While changeless measured change ; the spirit of prayer
Fanning that wondrous picture oft to flame
Until the glory grew insufferable.
Long years thus lived he.   As the Apostle Paul,
Though raised in raptures to the heaven of heavens,
Not therefore loved his brethren less, but longed
To give his life — his all — for Israel's sake, —
So Cuthbert, loving God, loved man the more,
His wont of old.   To him the mourners came,
And sinners bound by Satan.   At his touch
Their chains fell from them, light as summer dust.
Each word he spake was as a Sacrament
Clothed with God's grace ; beside his feet they sat,
And in their perfect mind ; thence through the world
Bare their deliverer's name.
                              So passed his life.
There old he grew, and older yet appeared,
By fasts outworn, though ever young at heart ;
When, lo ! before that isle a barge there drew,

Bearing the royal banner.  Egfrid, there,
With regal sceptre sat, and many an earl,
And many a mitred bishop at his side.
Northumbria's see was void ; a council's voice,
Joined with a monarch's, called him to its throne ;
In vain he wept, and knelt, and sued for grace ;
Six months' reprieve alone he won ; then ruled
In Lindisfarne, chief Bishop of the North.
     But certain spake who deemed that they were wise,
Fools all beside : " Shall Cuthbert crosier lift?
A child, 'tis known he herded flocks for hire,
Housed in old Renspid's hut, his Irish nurse,
Who told him tales of Leinster Kings, his sires,
And how her hands, their palace wrecked in war,
Had snatched him from its embers.  Yet a boy,
He rode to Melrose and its wondering monks,
A mimic warrior, in his hand a lance,
With shepherd youth for page, and spake : ' 'Tis
          known
Christ's kingdom is a kingdom militant :
A son of Kings, I come to guard His right,
And battle 'gainst his foes !'  For lance and sword
A book they gave him ; and they made him monk.
Savage since then he couches on a rock,
As fame reports, with birds' nests in his beard !
Can dreamers change to Bishops?  Vision-dazed,
Move where he may, that slowly wandering eye
Will see in man no more than kites or hawks ;
Men, if they note, will flee him."  Thus they buzzed,
Self-praised, and knowing not that simpleness

Is sacred soil, and sown with royal seed,
The heroic seed and saintly.
                              Mitred once,
Such gibes no more assailed him ; one short month
Sufficed the petty cavil to confute ;
One month well chronicled in book which verse
Late born, alas, in vain would emulate.
At once he called to mind the days that were ;
His wanderings in Northumbrian glens ; the hearths
That welcomed him so joyously ; at once
Within his breast the heart parental yearned ;
He longed to see his children, scattered wide
From Humber's bank to Tweed, from sea to sea,
And cried to those around him : "Let us forth,
And visit all my charge ; and since Carlisle
Remotest sits upon its western bound,
Keep there this year our Pentecost ! "   Next day
He passed the sands, left hard by ebbing tide,
His cross-bearer and brethren six in front,
And trod the mainland.   Reverent, first he sought
His childhood's nurse, and 'neath her humble roof
Abode one night.   To Melrose next he fared,
Honouring his master old.
                              Southward once more
Returning, scarce a bow-shot from the woods
There rode to him a mighty thane, one-eyed,
With warriors circled, on a jet-black horse,
Barbaric shape and huge, yet frank as fierce,
Who thus made boast : " A Jute devout am I !
What raised that convent-pile on yonder rock ?

This hand !   I wrenched the hillside from a foe
By force, and gave it to thy Christian monks
To spite yet more those Angles !   Island Saint,
Unprofitable have I found thy Faith !
Behold, those priests, thy thralls, are savage men,
Unrighteous, ruthless !   For a sin of mine
They laid on me a hundred days of fast !
A man am I keen-witted :  friend and liege
I summoned, showed my wrong, and ended thus :
'Sirs, ye are ninety-nine, the hundredth I ;
I counsel that we share this fast among us !
To-morrow, from the dawn to evening's star,
No food as bulky as a spider's tongue
Shall pass our lips ; and thus, in one day's time,
My hundred days of fast shall stand fulfilled.'
Wrathful they rose, and sware by Peter's keys
That fight they would, albeit 'gainst Peter's self ;
But fast they would not, save for personal sins.
Signal I made ; then backward rolled the gates,
And, captured thus, they fasted without thanks,
Cancelling my debt — a hundred days in one !
Beseech you, Father, chide your priests who breed
Contention thus 'mid friends !"   The Saint replied,
" Penance is irksome, Thane ; to 'scape its scourge
Ways are there various ; and the easiest this, —
Keep far from mortal sin."

                Where'er he faced,
The people round him pressed — the sick, the blind,
Young mothers sad because a babe was pale ;
Likewise the wives of fishers, praying loud

Their husbands' safe return.    Rejoiced he was
To see them, hear them, touch them ; wearied never ;
Whate'er they said, delighted still he heard ;
The rise and fall of empires touched him less,
The book rich-blazoned, or the high-towered church.
"We have," he said, "God's children, and their God ;
The rest is fancy's work." Him, too, they loved ;
Loved him the more because, so great and wise,
He stumbled oft in trifles.    Once he said, —
" How well those pine-trees shield the lamb from wind !"
A smile ran round ; at last the boldest spake, —
" Father, these are not pine-trees — these are oaks."
And Cuthbert answered,—"Oaks, good sooth, they are !
In youth I knew the twain apart : the pine
Wears on his head the Cross." Instruction next
He gave them, how the Cross had vanquished sin ;
Then first abstruse to some appeared his words.
" Father," they answered, "speak in parables !
For pleasant is the tale, and, onward passed,
Keeps in our hearts thy lesson."
                                 While they spake,
A youth rich-vested tossed his head and cried :
" Father, why thus converse with untaught hinds ?
Their life is but the life of gnats and flies ;
They think but of the hour.    Behold yon church !
I reared it both for reverence of thy Christ,
And likewise that through ages yet to come
My name might live in honour !" At that word
Cuthbert made answer : " Hear the parable !
My people craved for such.

                                    A monk there lived,
Holiest of men reputed.   He was first
On winter mornings in the freezing stall ;
Meekest when chidden ; fervent most in prayer ;
And, late in life, when heresies arose,
That book he wrote, like tempest winged from God,
Drave them to darkness back.   Grey-haired he died ;
With honour was interred.   The years went by ;
His grave they opened.   Peacefully he slept,
Unchanged, the smile of death upon his lips.
O'er the right hand alone, for so it seemed,
Had Death retained his power ; five little lines,
White ashes, showed where once the fingers lay.
All saw it — simple, learnèd, rich and poor ;
None might divine the cause.   That night, behold !
A Saintly Shape beside the abbot stood,
Bright like the sun, except one lifted palm —
Thereon there lay a stain.   ' Behold that hand,'
The Spirit spake, ' that, toiling twenty years,
Sent forth that book which pacified the world !
For it the world would canonise me Saint.
See that ye do it not !   Inferior tasks
I wrought for God alone.   Building that book,
Too oft I mused, — " Far years will give thee praise."
I expiate that offence.' "
                                    Another day,
A sweet-faced woman raised her voice, and cried, —
" Father ! those sins, denounced by God, I flee ;
Yet tasks, imposed by God, too oft neglect.
Stands thus a soul imperilled ? "   Cuthbert spake :
    M

" Ye sued for parables ; I speak in such,
Though ill — a language strange to me, and new.
There lived a man who shunned committed sin,
Yet daily by omission sinned, and knew it.
In his own way, not God's, he served his God ;
And there was with him peace ; yet not God's peace.
So passed his youth.   In age he dreamed a dream :
He dreamed that, being dead, he raised his eyes,
And saw a mountain range of frozen snows,
And heard, 'Committed sins innumerable
Though each one small — so small thou knew'st them
          not —
Uplifted, flake by flake as sin by sin,
Yon barrier 'twixt thy God and thee !   Arise,
Remembering that of sins despair is worst.
Be strong, and scale it !'   Fifty years he scaled
Those hills ; so long it seemed.   A cavern next
Entering, with mole-like hands he scooped his way,
And reached at last the gates of morn.   Ah me !
A stone's cast from him rose the Tree of Life ;
He heard its sighs ecstatic ; full in view
The Beatific River rolled ; beyond,
All-glorious, shone the City of the Saints,
Clothed with God's light !  And yet from him that realm
Was severed by a gulf !   Not wide that strait ;
It seemed a strong man's leap twice told — no more ;
But, as insuperably soared that cliff,
Unfathomably thus its sheer descent
Walled the abyss.   Again he heard that Voice :
' Henceforth, no place remains for active toils —

Penance for acts perverse.   Inactive sloth,
Through passive sufferings, meets its due.   On earth,
That sloth a nothing seemed ; a nothing now
That chasm, whose hollow bars thee from the Blest —
Poor slender film of insubstantial air.
Self-help is here denied thee ; for that cause
A twofold term thou need'st of pain love-taught
To expiate Love that lacked.'   That term complete,
An angel caught him o'er that severing gulf : —
Thenceforth, he saw his God."

                                            With such discourse
Progress, though slow and interrupted oft,
The Saint of God, by no delay perturbed,
Made daily through his sacred charge.   One eve
He walked by pastures arched along the sea,
With many companied.   The on-flowing breeze
Glazed the green hill-tops, bending still one way
The glossy grasses ; limitless below,
The ocean mirror, clipped by cape or point
With low trees inland leaning, lay like lakes
Flooding rich lowlands.   Southward far, a rock,
Touched by a rainy beam, emerged from mist,
And shone, half green, half gold.   That rock was Farne.
Though strangers, those that kenned it guessed its
      name.
" Doubtless 'twas there," they said, " our Saint abode ! "
Then pressed around him, questioning : " Rumour
      goes,
Father beloved, that in thine island home
Thou sat'st all day with hammer small in hand,

Shaping, from pebbles veined, miraculous beads
That save their wearers still from sword and lance : —
Are these things true ? "   Smiling the Saint replied :
" True, and not true !   That isle, in part, is spread
With pebbles divers-fashioned, some like beads.
I gathered such, and gave to many a guest,
Adding, — ' Such beads shall count thy nightly prayers ;
Pray well ; then fear no peril ! ' "
                                              Others came,
And thus demanded :  " Rumour fills the world,
Father, that birds miraculous crowned thine isle,
And, awe-struck, let thee lift them in thy hand,
Though scared by all beside."   Smiling once more,
The Saint made answer, — " True, and yet not true !
Sea-birds, elsewhere beheld not, throng that isle ;
A breed so loving, and so firm in trust,
That, yet unharmed by man, they flee not man ;
Wondering they gaze ; who wills may close upon them !
I signed a league betwixt that race and man,
Pledging the mariners who sought my cell
To reverence still that trust."   He ended thus :
" My friends, ye seek me still for parables ;
Seek them from Nature rather : — here are two !
Those pebble-beads are words from Nature's lips,
Exhorting man to pray ; those fearless birds
Teach him that trust to innocence belongs
By right divine, and more avails than craft
To shield us from the aggressor."   Some were glad,
Hearing that doctrine ; others cried, — " Not so !
Our Saint — all know it — makes miraculous beads ;

But, being humble, he conceals his might."
And, many an age, when slept that Saint in death,
Passing his isle by night the sailor heard
Saint Cuthbert's hammer clinking on the rock;
And, age by age, men cried, — " Our Cuthbert's birds
Revere the Saint's command."

                      While thus they spake.
A horseman over moorlands near the Tweed
Made hasty way, and thus addressed the Saint:
" Father, Queen Ermenburga greets thee well,
And this her message : — ' Queen am I forlorn,
Long buffeted by many a storm of state,
And worn at heart besides ; for in our house
Peace lived not inmate, but a summer guest ;
And now, my lord, the King is slain in fight ;
And changed the aspect, now, things wore of old.
Thou, therefore, man of God, approach my gates
With counsel sage.   This further I require ;
Thy counsel must be worthy of a Queen,
Nor aught contain displeasing.' "   Cuthbert spake :
" My charge requires my presence at Carlisle ;
Beseech the Queen to meet me near its wall
On this day fortnight."

                  Thitherwards, thenceforth,
Swiftlier he passed, while daily from the woods
The woodmen flocked, and shepherds from the hills,
Concourse still widening.   These among there moved
A hermit meek as childhood, calm as eld,
Long years Saint Cuthbert's friend.   Recluse he lived,
Within a woody isle of that fair lake

By Derwent lulled and Greta.   Others thronged
Round Cuthbert's steps ; that hermit stood apart,
With large dark eyes upon his countenance fixed,
And pale cheek dewed with tears.   The name he bore
Was " Herbert of the Lake."

                        Two weeks went by,
And Cuthbert reached his journey's end.   Next day,
God sent once more His Feast of Pentecost
To gladden men ; and all His Church on earth
Shone out, irradiate as by silver gleams
Flashed from her whiter Sister in the skies ;
And every altar laughed, and every hearth ;
And many a simple hind in spirit heard
The wind which, through that "upper chamber"
    swept,
Careering through the universe of God,
New life through all things poured.   Cuthbert, that
    day,
Borne on by wingèd winds of rapturous thought,
Forth from Carlisle had fared alone, and reached
Ere long a mead tree-girded ; — in its midst
Swift-flowing Eden raced from fall to fall,
Showering at times her spray on flowers as fair
As graced that earlier Eden ; flowers so light
Each feeblest breath impalpable to man
Now shook them and now swayed.   Delighted eye
The Saint upon them fixed.   Ere long he gazed
As glad on crowds thronging the river's marge,
For now the high-walled city poured abroad
Her children rich and poor.   At last he spake :

" Glory to Him Who made both flowers and souls !
He doeth all things well !   A few weeks past,
Yon river rushed by wintry banks forlorn ;
What decks it thus to-day?   The voice of Spring !
She  called  those  flowers  from  darkness  forth ;  she
    flashed
Her life into the snowy breast of each ;
This day she sits enthroned on each and all ;
The thrones are myriad ; but the Enthroned is One ! "
He paused ; then, kindling, added thus : " O friends !
'Tis thus with human souls through faith re-born.
One Spirit calls them forth from darkness ; shapes
One Christ, in each conceived, its life of life ;
One God finds rest, enthroned on all.   Once more,
The thrones are many, but the Enthroned is One ! "
Again he paused, and mused : again he spake :
" Yea, and in heaven itself, a hierarchy
There is, that glories in the name of ' Thrones.'
The high cherubic knowledge is not theirs ;
Not theirs the fiery flight of Seraph's love ;
But all their restful beings they dilate
To make a single, myriad throne for God.
Children, abide in unity and love !
So shall your lives be one long Pentecost,
Your hearts one throne for God ! "

                        As thus he spake
A breeze, wide-wandering through the woodlands near,
Illumed their golden roofs, while louder sang
The birds on every bough.   Then horns were heard
Resonant from stem to stem, from rock to rock,

While moved in sight a stately cavalcade
Flushing the river's crystal.   Of that host
Foremost and saddest Ermenburga rode,
A Queen sad-eyed, with large imperial front
By sorrow seamed ; a lady rode close by ;
Behind her, earls and priests.   Though proud to man,
Her inborn greatness made her meek to God.
She signed the Saint to stay not his discourse,
And placed her at his feet.

                         His words were great :
He spake of Pentecost ; no transient grace,
No fugitive act, consummated, then gone,
But God's perpetual presence in that Church
O'er-shadowed still, like Mary, by His Spirit,
Fecundated in splendour by His Truth,
Made loving through His Love.   The reign of Love
He showed, though perfected in Christ alone,
Not less co-eval with the race of man.
For what is man?   Not mind ; the beasts can think :
Not passions, appetites ; the beasts have these :
Nay, but Affections ruled by Laws Divine :
These make the life of man.   Of these he spake ;
Proclaimed of these the glory.   These to man
Are countless loves revealing Love Supreme ;
These and the Virtues, warp and woof, enweave
A single robe — that sacrificial garb
Worn from the first by man, whose every act
Of love in spirit was self-sacrifice,
And prophesied the Sacrifice Eterne ;
Through these the world becomes one household vast ;

Through these each hut swells to a universe
Traversed by stateliest energies wind-swift,·
And planet-crowned, beneath their Maker's eye.
All hail, Affections, angels of the earth !
Woe to that man who boasts of love to God,
And yet his neighbour scorns !   While Cuthbert spake
A young man whispered to a priest, " Is yon
That Anchoret of the rock ?   Where learned he, then,
This loving reverence for the hearth and home ?
Mark, too, that glittering brow ! "   The priest replied :
" What ! shall a bridegroom's face alone be bright ?
He knows a better mystery !   This he knows,
That, come what may, all o'er the earth forever
God keeps His blissful Bridal-feast with man.
Each true heart there is guest ! "
                                        Once more the Saint
Arose and spake : " O loving friends, my children,
Christ's sons, His flock committed to my charge !
I spake to you but now of humbler ties,
Not highest, with intent that ye might know
How pierced are earthly bonds by heavenly beam ;
Yet, speaking with lame tongue in parables,
I showed you but similitudes of things —
Twilight, not day.   Make question then who will ;
So shall I mend my teaching."
                                        Prompt and bright
As children issuing forth to holiday,
Then flocked to Cuthbert's school full many a man
Successive.   Each with simpleness of heart
His doubt propounded ; each his question asked,

Or, careless who might hear, confessed his sins,
And absolution won.   Among the rest,
A little seven years' boy, with sweet, still face,
Yet strong not less, and sage, drew softly near,
His great calm eyes upon the patriarch fixed,
And silent stood.   From Wessex came that boy ;
By chance Northumbria's guest.   Meantime a chief
Demanded thus : " Of all the works of might,
What task is worthiest ? "   Cuthbert made reply :
" His who to land barbaric fearless fares,
And open flings God's palace gate to all,
And cries ' Come in ! ' "   That concourse thrilled for
        joy ;
Alone that seven years' child retained the word ;
The rest forgat it.   " Winifrede," that day,
Men called him ; later centuries, " Boniface,"
Because he shunned the ill, and wrought the good.
In time the Teuton warriors knew that brow —
Their great Apostle he ; they knew that voice,
And happy Fulda venerates this day
Her martyr's gravestone.

                    Next, to Cuthbert drew
Three maidens, hand in hand, lovely as Truth,
Trustful, though shy ;   their thoughts, when hidden
        most,
Wore but a semilucid veil, as when,
Through gold-touched crystal of the lime new-leaved,
On April morns, the symmetry looks forth
Of branch and bough distinct.   Smiling, they put,
At last, their question : " Tell us, man of God,

What life, of lives that women lead, is best;
Then show us forth in parables that life!"
 He answered: "Three; for each of these is best.
First comes the Maiden's: she who lives it well
Serves God in marble chapel white as snow,
His priestess — His alone.   Cold flowers each morn
She culls ere sunrise by the stainless stream,
And lays them on that chapel's altar-stone,
And sings her matins there.   Her feet are swift
All day in labours 'mid the vales below,
Cheering sad hearts; each evening she returns
To that high fane, and there her vespers sings;
Then sleeps, and dreams of heaven."
       With witching smile,
The youngest of that beauteous triad cried:
"That life is sweetest!   I would be that maid!"
Cuthbert resumed: "The Christian Wife comes next:
She drinks a deeper draught of life; round her
In ampler sweep its sympathies extend;
An infant's cry has knocked against her heart,
Evoking thence that human love wherein
Self-love hath least.   Through infant eyes a spirit
Hath looked upon her, crying, — 'I am thine!
Creature from God — dependent yet on thee!'
Thenceforth, she knows how greatness blends with
  weakness;
Reverence, thenceforth, with pity linked, reveals
To her the pathos of the life of man —
A thing divine, and yet at every pore
Bleeding from crownèd brows.   A heart thus large

Hath room for many sorrows.    What of that?
Its sorrow is its dowry's noblest part.
She bears it not alone.    Such griefs, so shared —
Sickness, and fear, and vigils lone and long —
Waken her heart to love sublimer far
Than ecstasies of youth could comprehend ;
Lift her, perchance, to heights serene as those
The Ascetic treadeth."

                           " I would be that wife ! "
Thus cried the second of those maidens three.
Yet who that gazed upon her could have guessed
Creature so soft could bear a heart so brave?
She seemed that goodness which was beauteous too;
Virtue at once, and Virtue's bright reward ;
Delight that lifts, not lowers us ; made for heaven ; —
Made too to change to heaven some brave man's hearth
She added thus : " Of lives that women lead
Tell us the third ! "

                        Gently the Saint replied :
" The third is Widowhood — a wintry sound ;
And yet, for her who widow is indeed,
That winter something keeps of autumn's gold,
Something regains of Spring's first flower snow-white,
Snow-cold, and colder for its rim of green.
She feels no more the warmly-greeting hand ;
The eyes she brightened rest on her no more ;
Her full-orbed being now is cleft in twain ;
Her past is dead ; daily from memory's self
Dear things depart ; yet still she is a wife, —
A wife the more because of bridal bonds

Lives but their essence, waiting wings in heaven;—
More wife; and yet, in that great loneliness,
More maiden, too, than when first maidenhood
Lacked what it missed not.   Like that other maid,
She, too, a lonely Priestess serves her God;
Yea, though her chapel be a funeral vault,
Its altar black like Death;—the flowers thereon,
Tinct with the Blood Divine.   Above that vault
She hears the anthems of the Spouse of Christ,
Widowed, like her, though Bride."

　　　　　　　　　　　　　　" O fair, O sweet,
O beauteous lives, all three; fair lot of women!"
Thus cried again the youngest of those Three,
Too young to know the touch of grief—or cause it—
A plant too lightly leaved to cast a shade.
The eldest with pale cheek, and lids tear-wet,
Made answer sad: " I would not be a widow."

　　Then Cuthbert spake once more with smile benign:
" I said that each of these three lives is best:—
There are who live those three conjoined in one:
The nun thus lives!   What maid is maid like her
Who, free to choose, has vowed a maidenhood
Secure 'gainst chance or choice?   What bride like
　　　her
Whose Bridegroom is the spouse of vestal souls?
What widow lives in such austere retreat,
Such hourly thought of him she ne'er can join
Save through the gate of death?   If those three lives
In separation lived are fair and sweet,
How show they, blent in one?"

Of those who heard
The most part gladdened ; those who knew how high
Virtue, renouncing all besides for God,
Hath leave to soar on earth.   Yet many sighed,
Jealous for happy homesteads.   Cuthbert marked
That shame-faced sadness, and continued thus :
"To praise the nun reproaches not, O friends,
But praises best that life of hearth and home
At Cana blessed by Him who shared it not.
The uncloistered life is holy, too, and oft
Through changeful years in soft succession links
Those three fair types of woman ; holds, diffused,
That excellence severe which life, detached,
Sustains in concentration."   Long he mused ;
Then added thus : "When last I roved these vales,
There lived, not distant far, a blessed one,·
Revered by all ; her name was Ethelreda ;
I knew her long, and much from her I learned.
Beneath her Pagan father's roof there sat
Ofttimes a Christian youth.   With him the child
Walked, calling him 'her friend.'   He loved the maid ;
Still young, he drew her to the fold of Christ ;
Espoused her three years later ; died in war
Ere three months passed.   For her he never died !
Immortalised by faith that bond lived on ;
And now close by, and now 'mid Saints of heaven,
She saw her husband walk.   She never wept ;
That fire which lit her eye, and flushed her cheek,
Dried up, it seemed, her tears ; the neighbours round
Called her 'the lady of the happy marriage.'

She died long since, I doubt not."    Forward stepped
A slight, pale maid, the daughter of a bard,
And answered thus : "Two months ago she died."
Then Cuthbert : "Tell me, maiden, of her death ;.
And see you be not chary of your words,
For well I loved that woman."    Tears unfelt
Fast streaming down her pallid cheek, the maid
Replied — yet often paused : "A sad, sweet end !
A long night's pain had left her living still ;
I found her on the threshold of her door.
Her cheek was white ; but, trembling round her lips,
And dimly o'er her countenance spread, there lay
Something that, held in check by feebleness,
Yet tended to a smile.    A cloak, tight-drawn,
From the cold March wind screened her, save one hand
Stretched on her knee, that reached to where a beam,
Thin slip of watery sunshine, sunset's last,
Slid through the branches.    On that beam, methought,
Rested her eyes half-closed.    It was not so ;
For when I knelt, and kissed that hand ill-warmed,
Smiling she said : 'The small, unwedded maid
Has missed her mark !    You should have kissed the
    ring !
Full forty years upon a widowed hand
It holds its own.    It takes its latest sunshine.'
She lived through all that night, and died while dawned
Through snows Saint Joseph's morn."

                        The Queen, with hand
Sudden and swift, brushed from her cheek a tear ;
And many a sob from that thick-crowding host

Confessed what tenderest love can live in hearts
Defamed by fools as barbarous.   Cuthbert sat
In silence long.   Before his eyes she passed,
The maid, the wife, the widow, all in one ;
With these — through these — he saw once more the
      child,
Yea, saw the child's smile on the lips of death,
That magic, mystic smile !   O heart of man,
What strange capacities of grief and joy
Are thine !   How vain, how ruthless such, if given
For transient things alone !   O life of man !
What wert thou but some laughing demon's scoff,
If prelude only to the eternal grave !
" Deep cries to deep " — ay, but the deepest deep,
Crying to summits of the mount of God,
Drags forth for echo, " Immortality."
It was the Death Divine that vanquished death !
Shorn of that Death Divine, the Life Divine —
Albeit its feeblest tear had cleansed all worlds,
Cancelled all guilt — had failed to reach and sound
The deepest in man's nature, Love and Grief,
Profoundest each when joined in penitent woe ;
Failed thence to wake man's hope.   The loftiest light,
Flashed from God's Face on Reason's orient verge,
Answers that bird-cry from the *Heart* of man —
Poor Heart that, darkling, kept so long its watch —
The auspice of the dawn.

                    Like one inspired
The Saint arose, and raised his hands to God ;
Then to his people turned with such discourse

As mocks the hand of scribe.   No more he spake
In parables ; adumbrated no more
" Dimly as in a glass " his doctrine high,
But placed it face to face before men's eyes,
Essential truth, God's image, meet for man,
Himself God's image.   Worlds he showed them new,
Worlds countless as the stars that roof our night,
Fair fruitage of illimitable boughs,
Pushed from that Tree of Life from Calvary sprung
That over-tops and crowns the earth and man ;
Preached the Resurgent, the Ascended God,
Dispensing " gifts to men."   The tongue he spake
Seemed Pentecostal — grace of that high Feast —
For all who heard, the simple and the sage,
Heard still a single language sounding forth
To all one Promise.   From that careworn Queen,
Who doffed her crown, and placed it on the rock,
Murmuring, — " Farewell forever, foolish gaud,"
To him, the humblest hearer, all made vow
To live thenceforth for God.   The form itself
Of each was changed to saintly and to sweet ;
Each countenance beamed as though with rays cast
    down
From fiery tongues, or angel choirs unseen.
    Thus, like high gods on mountain-tops of joy,
Those happy listeners sat.   The body quelled —
With all that body's might usurped to cramp
Through ceaseless, yet unconscious, weight of sense
Conceptions spiritual, might more subtly skilled
Than lusts avowed, to sap the spirit's life —

N

In every soul its nobler Powers released
Stood up, no more a jarring crowd confused,
Each trampling each and oft the worst supreme, —
Not thus, but grade o'er grade, in order due,
And pomp hierarchical.   Yet hand in hand,
Not severed, stood those Powers.   To every Mind
That truth new learned was palpable and dear,
Not abstract nor remote, with cordial strength
Enclasped as by a heart ; through every Heart
Serene affections swam 'mid seas of light,
Reason's translucent empire without bound,
Fountained from God.   Silent those listeners sat,
Parleying in wordless thought.   For them the world
Was lost — and won ; its sensuous aspects quenched ;
Its heavenly import grasped.   The erroneous Past
Lay like a shrivelled scroll before their feet ;
And, sweet as some immeasurable rose,
Expanding leaf on leaf, varying yet one,
The Everlasting Present round them glowed.
Dead was desire, and dead not less was fear —
The fear of change — of death.

                               An hour went by ;
The sun declined ; then rising from his seat,
Herbert, the anchoret of the lonely lake,
Made humble way to Cuthbert's feet with suit:
"O Father, and O Friend, thou saw'st me not ;
Yet, day by day, thus far I tracked thy steps
At distance, for my betters leaving place,
The great and wise that round thee thronged ; the
    young

Who ne'er till then had seen thy face; the old
Who saw it then, yet scarce again may see.
Father, a happier lot was mine, thou know'st,
Or had been save for sin of mine : each year
I sought thy cell, thy words of wisdom heard;
Yet still, alas! lived on, like sensual men
Who yield their hearts to creatures — fixing long
A foolish eye on gold-touched leaf, or flower —
Not Him, the great Creator.  Father and Friend,
The years run past.  I crave one latest boon :
Grant that we two may die the self-same day!"
Then Cuthbert knelt, and prayed.  At last he spake :
"Thy prayer is heard; the self-same day and hour
We two shall die."

           That promise was fulfilled;
For two years only on exterior tasks
God set His servant's hands — the man who "sought
In all things rest," nor e'er had ceased from rest
Then when his task was heaviest.  Two brief years
He roamed on foot his spiritual realm;
The simple still he taught; the sad he cheered;
Where'er he went he founded churches still,
And convents; yea, and, effort costlier far,
Spared not to scan defect with vigilant eye.
That eye the boldest called not "vision-dazed;"
That Saint he found no "dreamer;" sloth or greed
'Scaped not his vengeance; scandals hid he not,
But dragged them into day, and smote them down;
Before his face he drave the hireling priest,
The bandit thane; unceasing cried, — "Ye kings,

Cease from your wars!    Ye masters, loose your
    slaves!"
Two years sufficed; for all that earlier life
Had trained the Ascetic for those works of might
Beyond the attempt of all but boundless love,
And in him kept unspent the fire divine.
Never such Bishop walked till then the North,
Nor ever since, nor ever, centuries fled,
So lived in hearts of men.    Two years gone by,
His strength decayed.    He sought once more his cell
Sea-lulled; and lived alone with God; and saw
Once more, like lights that sweep the unmoving hills,
God's providences girdling all the world,
With glory following glory.    Tenderer-souled,
Herbert, meantime, within his isle abode,
At midnight listening Derwent's gladsome voice
Mingling with deep-toned Greta's, "Mourner" named;
Pacing, each day, the shore; now gazing glad
On gold-touched leaf, or bird that cut the mere,
Now grieved at wandering thoughts.    For men he
    prayed;
And ever strove to raise his soul to God;
And God, Who venerates still the pure intent,
Forgat not his; and since his spirit and heart,
Holy albeit, were in the Eyes Divine
Less ripe than Cuthbert's for the Vision Blest —
Least faults perforce swelling where gifts are vast —
That God vouchsafed His servant sickness-pains
Virtue to perfect in a little space,
That both might pass to heaven the self-same hour.

It came : that sun, which flushed the spray up-hurled
In cloud round Cuthbert's eastern rock, while he
Within it dying chanted psalm on psalm,
Ere long enkindled Herbert's western lake ;
The splendour waxed ; mountain to mountain laughed,
And, brightening, nearer drew, and, nearing, clasped
That heaven-dropped beauty in more strict embrace ;
The cliffs successive caught their crowns of fire ;
Blencathara last.   Slowly that splendour waned ;
And, from the glooming gorge of Borrodale,
Her purple cowl shadowing her holy head
O'er the dim lake twilight with silent foot
Stepped like a spirit.   Herbert from his bed
Of shingles watched that sunset till it died ;
And at one moment from their distant isles
Those friends, by death united, passed to God.

# KING HENRY THE SECOND AT THE TOMB OF KING ARTHUR

## I

Why put the great in Time their trust?
    Whate'er on earth we prize
Of dust was made, and is but dust,
    For all its brave disguise.
No boor but one day with the just
    May triumph in the skies !

Ambition doth but chase a gleam ;
    An idle toy the sword !
The crown a mockery ; power a dream ;
    For Christ alone is Lord.
That lore King Henry learned.  Of him
    I here a tale record.

The tourney past, in festival
    Baron and knight were met ;
Last pomp it was that graced the hall
    Of great Plantagenet ;
A Prince for valour praised by all,
    More famed for wisdom yet.

The board rang loud with kingly cheer ;
    Light jest, and laugh, and song
Rang swiftly round from peer to peer ;

Alone, on that gay throng,
The harper looked with eye severe,
  The while in unknown tongue

A mournful dirge abroad he poured ;
  Sad strains, forlorn, and slow ;
Poor wreck of music prized and stored
  Long centuries ago
On British hills ere Saxon sword
  Had stained as yet their snow.

" Strike other chords," the monarch cried ;
  " Whate'er thy words may be,
They sound the dirge of festal pride ;
  Warriors, not monks are we !
The melodies to grief allied
  No music make for me."

The harper's eye with martial fire
  One moment shone ; no more ;
His lips, but now compressed in ire,
  A smile disdainful wore,
While forth from each resounding wire
  Its fiercer soul he tore.

Louder and louder pealed the strain,
  More wild, and soul-entrancing ;
Picturing now helmets cloven in twain ;
  Now swords like meteors glancing ;
Now trampling hosts o'er hill and plain
  Retreating and advancing.

Each measure, mightier than the last,
    Rushed forth, stern triumphs wooing ;
Like some great angel on the blast
    From heaven to heaven pursuing,
With outspread pinion, far and fast,
    A host abhorred to ruin.

The bard meanwhile with cold, stern air,
    Looked proudly on the proud,
Fixing unmoved a victor's stare
    On that astonished crowd —
'Till all the princes gathered there
    Leaped up, and cried aloud :

" What man, what chief, what crownèd head,
    Eternal heir of fame,
Of all that live, or all the dead,
    This praise shall dare to claim ? " —
Then rose that British bard, and said,
    " King Arthur is his name."

" What sceptre grasped King Arthur's hand ? "
    " The sceptre of this Isle."
" What nations bled beneath his brand ? "
    " The Saxon foe erewhile."
" His tomb ? " was Henry's next demand —
    " He sleeps in yonder pile."

Forth went the King with all his train,
    At the mid hour of night ;
They paced in pairs the silent plain

Under the red torch-light.
The moon was sinking in her wane,
   The tower yet glimmered bright.


## II

Through Glastonbury's cloister dim
   The midnight winds were sighing;
Chanting a low funereal hymn
   For those in silence lying,
Death's gentle flock, 'mid shadows grim
   Fast bound, and unreplying.

Hard by, the monks their Hours were saying;
   The organ evermore,
Its wave in alternation swaying,
   On that smooth swell upbore
The voice of their melodious praying
   Towards heaven's eternal shore.

Ere long a princely multitude
   Moved on 'neath arches grey,
Which yet, though shattered, stand where stood
   (God grant they stand for aye !)
Saint Joseph's church of woven wood
   On England's baptism day.

The grave they found ; their swift strokes fell,
   Piercing dull earth and stone.
They reached ere long an oaken cell,

And cross of oak, whereon
Was graved : "Here sleeps King Arthur well,
  In the Isle of Avalon."

The mail on every knightly breast,
  The steel at each man's side,
Sent forth a sudden gleam ; each crest
  Bowed low its plumèd pride ;
Down o'er the coffin stooped a priest —
  But first the monarch cried :

" Great King ! in youth I made a vow
  Earth's mightiest son to greet ;
His hand to worship ; on his brow
  To gaze ; his grace entreat.
Therefore, though dead, till noontide thou
  Shalt fill my royal seat ! "

Away the massive lid they rolled —
  Alas ! what found they there?
No kingly brow, no shapely mould ;
  But dust where such things were.
Ashes o'er ashes, fold on fold —
  And one bright wreath of hair.

Genevra's hair ! like gold it lay ;
  For Time, though stern, is just,
And humblest things feel last his sway,
  And Death reveres his trust. —
They touched that wreath ; it sank away
  From sunshine into dust !

Then Henry lifted from his head
  The Conqueror's iron crown ;
That crown upon that dust he laid,
  And knelt in reverence down,
And raised both hands to heaven, and said,
  " Thou, God, art King alone !

" Lie there, my crown, since God decrees
  This head a couch as low !
What am I better now than these
  Six hundred years ago ?
Henceforth, all mortal pageantries
  I count an idle show."

Such words King Henry spake ; and ere
  The cloistral vaults had felt
Along their arches dark and bare
  The last faint echo melt,
The nobles congregated there
  On that cold pavement knelt.

And each his coronet down laid,
  And Christ, his King, adored ;
And murmured in that mournful shade :
  " Thou, God, alone art Lord :
Like yonder hair at last shall fade
  Each sceptre, crown, and sword."

# THE INFANT BRIDAL

OF old between two nations was great war:
    Its cause no mortal knew; nor when begun;
Therefore they combated so much the more,
    The sire his sword bequeathing to the son;
Till gentleness and joy had wholly fled,
And well-nigh every hand with blood was red.

In vain the mother wept; her sighs were blown
    Away by the loud gust of popular rage;
In vain the young fair widow made her moan;
    In vain the tender virgin would engage
Her love to gentler thoughts; he rushed to arms,
Proud of her beauty pale and loud alarms.

Glory, for Honour a blind substitute
    In hearts aspiring and a servile will,
On to the battle chased them.   Man and brute,
    Horseman and horse, by the same trumpet-thrill
Were borne into the frenzy of red fields,
Ghastly ere night with dead, upstaring from their
        shields.

Glory at first, and after Glory, Shame;
    Shame to propose the compact, first to bend;
And Fear, which masks full oft in Valour's name,

And doth false honour like a shade attend —
Fear to be thought to fear ; — these plagues did urge
The maniacs forward with a threefold scourge.

Both kingdoms raging thus in fever fit,
　More direful every hour became their spleen;
The sleeping boy full oft his brow would knit
　Against a foeman he had never seen;
Full oft the man of venerable hairs
Bowed to the dust his head depressed by griefs and
　　cares.

Valley and town lay drowned in tears and sorrow;
　Each noontide trembled with perturbed annoy,
And no one dared expect a kinder morrow;
　To be a mother was no more a joy;
Hope no more hovered o'er the cradle.　Love
Wept; and no friend had heart such anguish to re-
　　prove.

How often to a little sleeping child,
　Smiling, and sleeping on the mother's knee,
That mother thus complained: "Ah, little child!
　God only knows if it be good for thee,
My comforter, my solace, to have come
Down to this world so harsh and wearisome.

"Happy awhile with me thy spirit dwells;
　Awhile contented 'mid thy petty range
Of daily things, to thee all miracles;
　For arms thou dost not sigh, nor pant for change;

Thy dreams are bloodless; thou dost smile when
    sleeping,
In Eden founts thy newborn fancies steeping.

"Ah, must that brow, so clear, so smooth, so white,
    By a hard ruthless helm be one day pressed?
Ah, must the red lance in its murderous might
    One day pierce through and gore that tender breast?
Ah, little infant! must thou lie one day
Far, far from me, cold clay upon cold clay?

"Wherefore so fast do these thy ringlets grow?
    Stay, little child, be alway what thou art,
That I may ever, while the rough winds blow,
    Clasp thee as now, and hide thee in my heart.
Who taught thee those new words?  I fear each day,
To hear thee cry, 'Mother, I must away.'

"Is this to be a mother?  I am none —
    And yet I fear to lose a gift not prized.
Is this, ah God, to have a little son?
    Are these my prayers? my dreams thus realised?
Defrauded of my own while visibly here,
How can I hope, O child, to deck far off thy bier?"

II

The hosts, in silence marching all the night,
    At sunrise met upon the battle plain.
The monarchs there engaged in single fight:
    There by a rival's hand was either slain.

Long time men stood in gloom, stern, and sad-
      hearted;
Then, bound by solemn vows, homeward in peace
      departed.

A counsel went there forth.   Each king had left
    Behind a blooming infant; one a boy,
A girl the other; both alike bereft;
    Both innocent; both mete for love and joy;
Both heirs of sorrow.   "Holy Church these twain
Shall join in one," men cried, "and peace be ours
      again."

Who first devised the expedient no one knows.
    Perhaps old sages, after long debate,
And loud lament of immemorial woes,
    Bending their deep brows in a hall of state,
Conceived the project; and from Fancy sought
A cure for ills by rage fantastic wrought.

Some chief perhaps, of all his sons bereft,
    And now half blind in his forlorn old age,
Cried loud in anguish, while his tower he left
    To hide him in a moss-grown hermitage, —
"Hear ye my words, and on your hearts engrain them,
Love gave me many children: Hate hath slain them."

Haply some maiden, for the war deserted,
    Exclaimed, — "I would that little warlike pair
Had loved as long as war the loved hath parted."
    Perhaps kind angels called her wish a prayer.

Enough : I tell an ancient legend, told
By better men than I, long dead and cold.

While the young bride in triumph home was led,
  They strewed beneath her litter branches green;
And kissed light flowers, then rained them on a head
  Unconscious as the flowers what all might mean.
Men, as she passed them, knelt; and women raised
Their children in their arms, who laughed and gazed.

That pomp approaching woodland villages,
  Or shadowing convents piled near rivers dim,
The church-bells from grey towers begirt with trees
  Reiterated their loud, wordless hymn;
And golden cross, and snowy choir serene
Moved on, old trunks and older towers between.

An hour ere sunset from afar they spied
  The city walls, dark myriads round them clinging;
Now o'er a carpeted expanse they glide,
  Now the old bridge beneath their tread is ringing;
They reach the gate — they pass the towers below —
And now once more emerge, a glittering show!

O what a rapturous shout receives them, blending
  Uncounted bells with chime of human voices!
That fortress old, as on they wind ascending,
  Like the mother of some victor chief rejoices.
From every window tapestries wave; among
The steep and glittering roofs, group after group, they
        throng.

The shrine is gained.   Two mighty gates expanding
   Let forth a breeze of music onward gushing,
In pathos lulled, yet awful and commanding;
   Down sink the crowds, at once their murmur hush-
       ing.
Filled with one soul, the smooth procession slowly
Advances with joined palms, cross-led and lowly.

Lo! where they stand in yon high, fan-roofed cham-
       ber —
   Martyrs and Saints in dyed and mystic glass
With sumptuous halos, vermeil, green and amber,
   Flood the far aisles, and all that by them pass:
Rich like their painter's visions — in those gleams
Blazoning the burden of his Patmian dreams!

A forest of tall lights in mystic cluster
   Like fire-topped reeds, from their aerial station,
Pour on the group a mild and silver lustre;
   Beneath the blessing of that constellation
The rite proceeds — pure source whence rich increase
Of love henceforth, and piety and peace.

Small was the ring, and small in truth the finger!
   What then? the faith was large that dropped it
      down;
A faith that scorned on this base earth to linger,
   And won from Heaven a perdurable crown.
A germ of Love, at plighting of that troth,
Into each bosom sank; and grew there with its growth.

   o

The ladies held aloft the bridal pair;
 They on each other smiled, and gazed around
With lofty mien benign and debonair,
 Their infant brows with golden circlet bound;
The prelates blessed them, and the nobles swore
True faith and fealty by the swords they bore.

Home to the palace, still in order keeping,
 That train returned; and in the stateliest room
Laid down their lovely burden, all but sleeping,
 Together in one cradle's curtained gloom;
And lulled them with low melody and song,
And jest passed lightly 'mid the courtly throng.

### III

Ah, lovely sight! behold them — creatures twain,
 Hand in hand wandering through some verdant
  alley,
Or sunny lawn of their serene domain,
 Their wind-caught laughter echoing musically;
Or skimming, in pursuit of bird-cast shadows,
With feet immaculate the enamelled meadows.

Tiptoe now stand they by some towering lily,
 And fain would peer into its snowy cave;
Now, the boy bending o'er some current chilly,
 The feebler backward draws him from the wave;
But he persists, and gains for her at last
Some bright flower from the dull weeds hurrying past.

Oft if some agèd priest the cloister crossed,
    Both hands they caught; and bade him explicate,
That nought of good through idlesse might be lost,
    At large all duties of the nuptial state;
And oft each other kissed with infant glee,
As though this were some great solemnity.

In some old missal sometimes would they look,
    Touching with awe the illuminated page;
And scarce for tears the spectacle might brook
    Of babes destroyed by Herod's murderous rage.
Here sank a Martyr in ensanguined vest;
With more familiar smile, there beamed the Virgin
      blest.

Growing, their confidence as quickly grew;
    Light pet and childish quarrel seldom came;
To make them lighter yet and yet more few,
    Their nurse addressed them thus—an ancient
      dame—
"Children, what perfect love should dwell, I ween,
'Twixt husband and young wife, 'twixt King and
      Queen.

"The turtle, widowed of her mate, no more
    Lifts her lone head, but pines, and pining dies;
In many a tomb 'mid yon Cathedral hoar
    Monarch or Knight beside his lady lies;
Such tenderness and truth they showed that fate
No power was given their dust to separate.

"Rachel not less, and Ruth, whereof men read
   In book ordained our life below to guide,
Loved her own husband each, in word and deed,
   Loved him full well, nor any loved beside;
And Orpheus too, and Pyramus, men say,
Though Paynim born, lived true, and so shall live
      for aye.


"What makes us, children, to good Angels dear?
   Unblemished Truth and hearts in pure accord.
These also draw the people to revere
   With stronger faith their King and Sovereign Lord.
Then perfect make your love and amity
Alway; but most of all if men are by."


Such lore receiving ofttimes, hand in hand
   Those babes walked gravely; at the garden gates
Meantime the multitude would flock and stand,
   And hooded nuns looked downward from their
      grates.
These when the Princes marked, they moved awhile
With loftier step and more majestic smile;


Or sat enthroned upon some broidered bank
   (The lowlier flowers in wrecks around them thrown)
Shadowed with roses rising rank on rank;
   And there, now wreathed, now leaning into one,
They talked, and kissed, again and yet again,
To please good Angels thus, and win good men.

Swift rolled the years.   The boy now twelve years old,
   Vowed to the Cross and honourable war,
For Palestine deserts our northland cold.
   Her husband — playmate — is he hers no more?
Up to his hand, now timid first she crept, —
"Farewell," he said; she sighed; he kissed her and
      she wept.

A milk-white steed; a crest, whose snowy pride
   Like wings, or maiden tresses, drooped apart;
A Cross between; and (every day new dyed)
   Fair emblem on his shield, a bleeding heart, —
Marked him far off from all.   Not mine to tell
What fields his valour won, what foes before him
      fell.

No barbarous rage that host impelled; but zeal
   For Christian faith and sacred rites profaned;
And Triumph smiled upon the avenging steel
   That smote the haughty and set free the chained.
Foremost he fought.   In Victory's final hour,
Star-bright, he shone from Salem's topmost tower!

Swift as that Fame, which like an Angel ran
   Before him on a glory-smitten road,
Homeward the princely boy returned, a man.
   A lovelier angel graced their old abode —
But where his youthful playmate? where?   Half dazed,
Each on the other's beauty wondering gazed.

Strange joy they found all day in wandering over
  The spots in which their childish sports had been;
Husband and wife whilome, now loved and lover,
  A broken light brightened yet more the scene.
Night came: a gay yet startled bride he led,
Old rites scarce trusting, to the bridal bed.

No more remains of all this ancient story.
  They loved with love eternal; spent their days
In peace, in good to man, in genuine glory;
  No spoils unjust they sought, nor unjust praise.
Their children loved them and their people blessed —
God grant us all such lives — in Heaven for aye such
        rest!

# SAINT FRANCIS AND PERFECT JOY

FROM THE FIORETTI DI S. FRANCESCO

BLESSED Saint Francis, in the winter time,
   When half the Umbrian vales were white with snow
And all the northward vine-stems rough with rime,
   Walked from Perugia down.  His steps were slow,
Made slow by thought; yet swift at times, for love
Showered o'er his musings, fired them from above.

Right opposite, high on Assisi's hill,
   The Saint was born, child of a wealthy house;
And though, corrupt delights abhorring still,
   The revel he had shunned, and wild carouse,
Not less in camps and 'mid the festal throng
At times the youth had lived; yet not for long.

For from the Eternal Altar in the skies
   The Kingly Prophet and the Victim Priest,
Standing with hands outstretched, had bent His eyes
   One moment on him.  Straight, from earth released,
The Saint, predestined, cast her lures aside,
And Holy Poverty espoused — his Bride.

Love, perfect made, lives in the Loved alone;
   All gifts, by him unshared, it spurns as dross;
He, Who for earth's sake left His heavenly throne,
   From earth accepted one sole gift — the Cross:

That day Saint Francis on that Cross and Him
Mused ever, as he walked, with eyes tear-dim.

At last thus spake he to that Brother meek,
    For hours sole comrade of his silent way:
" Leone, lamb of Christ, the words I speak
    Write down, and ponder well some far-off day;
For truth remains; but men are winds that pass,
Like those brief gusts that bend yon stiffening grass.

" Leone, we, the least of men, have striven
    An Order to uprear of Orders least;
If God, who ofttimes from His feast hath driven
    The proud, and shared Himself the beggar's feast,
Should dower that new-born Order with such grace
That one day it shall stand the first in place;

"If, in each land, the Brothers Minor shone
    Resplendent with a sanctity so high
That all men thronged to hear their word, and none
    Who heard in mortal sin was known to die,
All crowns of earth to this were but a toy;
Yet write that this would not be Perfect Joy."

Another mile that road ice-filmed they trod
    While sank the sun, and 'gainst their faces blew
Bitterer the blast; then stood the man of God,
    And thus with kindling cheek began anew:
" Leone, little lamb of Christ, attend !
Write down my words, and inly apprehend.

" Leone, if through all the earth in fear
   Before the Brothers Minor demons fled;
If in all lands they caused the deaf to hear,
   The blind to see, and raised the buried dead,
All this, though greatness proof 'gainst Time's
      alloy
And clear from stain, would not be Perfect Joy."


Again pushed on the twain through vapours frore
   And wayside boughs curdled with frozen rain;
But now Leone paced the Saint before,
   And oft his whitening fingers chafed for pain;
Again Saint Francis stood; and, with a mien
As though the Vision Blest his eyes had seen,


Resumed, but louder: " Little lamb, give ear!
   Write thus, that if the Brothers Minor flung
All nets of knowledge round the spiritual sphere
   And spake once more each Pentecostal tongue,
And depth on depth in Scripture hid explored,
And dragged the Soldan bound to Christ, his Lord;


" If, lastly, through all realms they sped His Faith
   Triumphant as on Angels' necks and wings,
And raised in Holy Land from shame and scath
   His just ones, abjects now of turbaned Kings,
Potent alone to abase and to destroy,
These things, though great, would not be Perfect
      Joy."

When three times now Leone thus had heard
  From lips so loved the self-same oracle,
He stood in wide-eyed wonder without word.
  At last he spake: "I pray thee, Father, tell
What thing is Perfect Joy; how won? where found?
In heaven, do Angels share it with the Crowned?"


Blessèd Saint Francis raised his thin, small hand
  And pointed to a chapel, now not far,
That lonely rose amid the dusking land,
  Backed by the dull red sky and evening star;
Scarce larger than a huge tree's hollow bole
That chapel seemed, their day-long journey's goal.


"Saint Mary of the Angels" it was named;
  That Order, destined soon o'er earth to spread,
As yet no statelier Mother-House had claimed;
  Four hermits grey from Palestine, men said,
Long centuries past, those sacred walls had reared;
Though time-worn, still they stood by all revered.


Round them not yet had risen that temple, graced
  With countless spoils from quarry and from mine,
Which clasps this hour, 'mid splendours undisplaced,
  That precinct old, its boast, its joy, its shrine,
Delight of pilgrim bands that, year by year,
Seeking its pardoning grace in faith draw near.

Still toward that spot the Saint held forth his hand —
 Ere long a cloud of mingled sleet and snow,
That seemed, as on it drifted, to expand,
 Drew nearer to that humble fane and low.
It passed; and plainly in the lessening light
Shone out the chapel, now with snow-flakes white.


Then spoke the Saint: "Leone, seest thou there
 Our happy home? If we who left it late
So bright, so glad, so silent, and so fair,
 Should cower snow-clad ere Compline by its gate,
And sue admittance, crying, — 'Porter, wake!
Receive thy Brethren for the Master's sake!'


"And if that porter, loth to leave his bed,
 Should answer from within, — 'Imposters base!
Come ye to gorge the olives and the bread
 Reserved for orphans and the sick? give place!
This knotted staff for backs like yours were best.
Hence! Psalms are over, and the Brethren rest:' —


"And if, an hour gone by, once more we came,
 And prayed: 'Great Sir, unbar to us the door;
Two Brothers Minor, spent, thy pity claim,
 Wanderers way-worn, heart-weary, and foot-sore;'
And he made answer: 'Hence! for, though I sleep,
For bandits masked my wolf-hounds vigil keep:' —

"And if, two hours gone by, again we sued,
   And forth that porter rushed with staff and hound,
Doubtless not knowing us in his Cain-like mood,
   And left us on the snows, bleeding and bound,
Till now on the blank road the morning shone,
And we at heart had cherished petulance none,

"Nor uttered contumelious word the while,
   But mused all night on Christ and on His Cross,
And thanked Him that He deigned with us, though
     vile,
   To share it, gain supreme disguised in loss,
And endless bliss won by an hour's annoy, —
Leone, Brother, that were Perfect Joy.

"Leone!   That, and every grace beside,
   Is gift of God, to nought man boasts akin;
Great sin it were, to turn God's gifts to pride: —
   *This* gift, slaying self-love, forestalls such sin!
Well cried the Apostle, pain-emparadised, —
'Glory in this I will — the Cross of Christ.'"

Hail, silent, chaste, and ever sacred stars!
Ye bind my life in one! I well remember
When first your glory pierced my youthful heart.
'Twas Christmas Eve near midnight. From a boat
I watched you long; then, rowing, faced the deep;
Above the storm-loved cliff of Elsinore
Sworded Orion high and higher rose
With brightening belt. The city clocks struck twelve;
Straight from the countless towers rang out their
    chimes,
Hailing the Babe new-born. Along the sea
Vibration waved; and in its depth the stars
Danced as they flashed, answering that rapturous
    hymn, —
"Glory to God on high and peace on earth."
I shall not long behold them, saith my leech.
He errs; I suffer little.
                On my bed
Yon lies my tome — one man's bequest to men.
Is the gift good? From youth to age I toiled,
A gleaner in the starry harvest field —
Lo, there one gathered sheaf!
I think I laboured with a stainless aim,
If not a single aim. In ancient times
Pythagoras had gleams of this high lore;
Let coming ages stamp his name upon it;
I count it his, not mine.

                              My earlier book
In substance was as this.    But thus I mused:
Christ's simple ones may take offence and cry, —
" 'Tis written, 'God hath made the earth so strong
That it cannot be moved '; Science avers
It moves around the sun."    Such questioner
Deserves all reverence.    Faith is more than Science;
But 'twixt the interpretation and the text
Lies space world-wide.    That text meant this — no
      more —
So solid is the earth, concussion none,
Though mountains fell, can move it.    Here is naught
Of motion round the sun.    Solidity
To such advance were needful, not a bar;
Far flies the pebble forward flung; the flower
Drops at the flinger's foot.
                              Again I mused:
The Truth of Nature with the Truth Revealed
Accords perforce; not so the illusive gloss,
By Nature's scholiasts forced on Nature's page.
That gloss of Ptolemy's made great Nature lie
A thousand years and more.    Through countless errors,
Thus only, Science feels her way to Truth.
May I not err like Ptolemy?    Distrustful,
I hid my book for thirty years and six,
Cross-questioning with fresh inquest patient skies,
And found there nothing that arraigned my lore,
Much that confirmed it.    From the Minster tower,
Canon that time at Warnia though unworthy,
I made my charts of angle, sine, and arc.

Those vigils left my feet so numbed at morn
They scarce could find the altar-step, my hands
Scarce lift the chalice! Day by day I prayed
With adjuration added, — "If, my God,
Thou seest my pride suborn my faculties,
Place me a witless one among those witless
That beg beneath church porches." Likewise I sued
The poor beside whose beds I ministered —
For their sake I had learned the healing craft —
To fence me with their prayers.

       Discovered truths
I blabbed not to the crowd, but told the wise, —
Such men as raised our stateliest fanes. In these
I found amazement less than I presaged.
There seemed a leaning in the minds of men,
As when a leaning cornfield shows the wind,
To such results as in Bologna's schools
Made way when there I dwelt. I note this day
The ecclesiastics of the higher sort
Are with me more than those whose lore is Nature;
These hate the foot that spurns prescription's fence;
Not so my friend, the bishop of old Kulm;
He cries, — "Go forward!" Thirty years ago
Milan's famed painter — he of the "Last Supper" —
Whispered me thus, — "The earth goes round the sun."
There are whose guess is prophecy.

        This night
I make election: twofold choice is mine;
The first, to hurl this book on yonder sea;
The last, to fling it on a flood more vast

And fluctuating more — the mind of man,
Crying, — "Fare forth, and take what God shall send!"
One doubt alone remains; no text it touches, —
But dangers from within.   In days gone by,
Near me a youth beside a casement stood,
The sea not distant and a heaven all stars;
Christ's Advent was our theme.   He cried, — "Look
      forth!
Yon skies confute the old Faith!   When Earth was
      young,
Wistful as lovers, credulous as children,
Men deemed that Earth the centre of the world,
The stars its lackeys and its torch-bearers.
Such science is foredoomed; mankind will learn
This sphere is not God's ocean, but one drop
Showered from its spray.   Came God from heaven
      for that?
Speak no more words!"
                              That was a tragedy!
A mood may pass; yet moods have murdered souls.
It proved not thus with him.   I looked again;
That face was as an angel's; from his brow
The cloud had passed.   Reverent, I spake no word;
Later, albeit at times such moods recurred,
That man was helpful to a nation's soul;
In death he held the Faith.
                              This Earth too small
For Love Divine!   Is God not Infinite?
If so, His Love is infinite.   Too small!
One famished babe meets pity more from man

Oft than an army slain! Too small for Love!
Was Earth too small to be by God created?
Why, then, too small to be redeemed?

                        The sense
Sees greatness only in the sensuous greatness.
Science in that sees little; Faith sees naught.
The small, the vast, are tricks of earthly vision;
To God, that Omnipresent All-in-Each,
Nothing is small, is far.

                   More late I knew
A hoary man, dim-eyed, with restless hands,
A zealot, barbed with jibe and scoff still launched
At priests and kings and holy womanhood;
One night descending from my tower he spake:
"A God, and God incarnate but for man,
That reasoning beast — and all yon glittering orbs
In cold obstruction left!"

                  Diverse those twain!
That youth, though dazzled by the starry vastness
And thus despising earth, had awe for God;
That grey-haired fool believed in matter only.
Compassion for those starry races robbed
By earth, like Esau, of their birthright just,
Is pretext. They that know not of a God, —
How know they that the stars have habitants?
'Tis Faith and Hope that spread delighted hands
To such belief; no formal proof attests it.
Concede them peopled; can the sophist prove
Their habitants are fallen? That too admitted,
Who told him that redeeming foot divine

P

Ne'er trod those spheres?   That fresh assumption
    granted,
What then?   Is not the Universe a whole?
Doth not the sunbeam herald from the sun
Gladden the violet's bosom?   Moons uplift
The tides; remotest stars lead home the lost;
Judæa was one country, one alone;
Not less Who died there, died for all.   The Cross
Brought help to buried nations; Time opposed
No bar to Love; why, then, should Space oppose one?
We know not what Time is, nor what is Space; —
Why dream that bonds like theirs can bind the
    Unbounded?
If Earth be small, likelier it seems that Love,
Compassionate most and condescending most
To Sorrow's nadir depths, should choose that Earth
For Love's chief triumph, missioning thence her gift
Even to the utmost zenith!

### To the Soul

Far more than to the intellect of man
I deemed the gift vouchsafed when on me first
This new-born Science dawned.   I said, "Long since
We call God *infinite;* what means that term?
A boy, since childhood walled in one small field,
Could answer nothing.   He who looks on skies
Ablaze with stars, not hand-maids poor of earth,
But known for worlds of measureless bulk and swift-
    ness,
Has mounted to another grade of spirit, —
Proceeded man.   The stars do this for man;

They make Infinitude *imaginable*.
God, by our instincts felt as infinite,
When known becomes such to our total being,
Mind, spirit, heart, and soul.  The greater Theist
Should make the greater Christian.  Yet, 'tis true
Best gifts may come too soon.

                       No marvel this:
The earth was shaped for myriad forms of greatness,
As Freedom, Genius, Beauty, Science, Art,
Some extant, some to be.  Such forms of greatness
Are, through God's will, greatness conditional.
Where Christ is greatest, these are great; elsewhere,
Great only to betray.  Sweetly and sagely,
In order grave, the Maker of all Worlds
Still modulates the rhythm of human progress;
His angels, on whose song the seasons float,
Keep measured cadence; all good things keep time,
Lest Good should strangle Better.  Aristotle
Aspired like me to base on fact and proof
Nature's philosophy.  Fate said him nay;
That Fate was kindness hidden.
The natural science of great Aristotle
Died young; his logic lived and helped the Church
To map her Christian Science.

                      Ancient Thought
And Christian Faith, opposed in most beside,
Held Man in reverence, each.  Much came of that;
Matter dethroned, a place remained for spirit;
Old Grecian song called Man creation's lord;
The Christian Creed named him his Maker's Image;

One was a humble reverence; one a proud;
Science that day perhaps had made men prouder;
The Ptolemaic scheme had place and use
Till Christian Faith, conquering the earth, had
    crowned it;
The arch complete, its centring is removed;
That Faith, which franchised first the soul of man,
Franchises next his mind.
                Another knowledge,
Man's appanage, now was snatched awhile from men,—
The Lore of antique ages said or sung:
It rolled, a river through the Athenian vales;
It sank, as though by miracle, in earth;
A fount, unsealed by hand divine, it leaps
Once more against the sun.
              That strange new birth
Had place when first I trod Italian soil.
Men spake of bards to Dante's self unknown,
To Francis, Bernard, Dominic, Aquinas.
Great Albert knew them not.   The oracles
Of lying gods were dumb; but dumb not less
The sage Greek poets, annalists, orators,
For God had uttered voice, and leaned from heaven,
Waiting the earth's response.   The air was mute,
Mute for the Saviour God had breathed it late,
Left it His latest sigh.   The ages passed.
Alone were Apostolic voices heard;
Then Fathers of the Church; the Schoolmen last.
Clamour surceased; the "Credo," for that cause,
Was plainlier heard. The winds and waves had fallen;

And there was a great calm — stillness of spirit
At heart of storm extern.   At last God's Truth
Had built o'er earth the kingdom of God's Peace.
Then penance-time was passed; Greece spake once
     more;
What was that speech but prophecy fulfilled, —
"The heathen shall become thy heritage?"
Euphrates and Ilissus flow again;
Grey wastes with roses flame.  New greatness nears us;
Shall not God's angels reap two harvest fields
Severing the wheat from tares?
                  Severance is needful,
 Yea, needfuller yet will prove as ages pass.
The nobler songs of Greece divulged in verse
Such Truths as Nature had retained though fallen,
Man's heart had prized.   Ay, but with these there
     mixed
Music debasing.   Christendom this day
Confronts two gifts, and trials likewise twain;
She must become the mother of great Nations;
Each Nation with the years will *breed* its Book,
Its Bible uninspired.   But if these Books
Should prove but sorcerers' juggling wares, these
     prophets
Stand up false prophets and their word a lie,
A voice from those two Books of Greece and Rome
Will sound their sentence, crying: "In the night
We sang sweet songs, the auguries of dawn;
We sang the Mother-land, the household loves,
The all-reverend eld, the virgin sanctitude,

The stranger's right, the altar reared to Pity;
Ye, 'mid the noontide glories turned to black,
Outshamed our worst with worse."

                            Should that voice peal,
Woe to the Nations which have sinned that sin!
Truth's golden bowl will at the cistern break,
Song's daughters be brought low.

                           For these two gifts —
The Science new, the Old Lore revived — the time
Seems opportune alike.  The earth finds rest.
That Rome which warred on Christ is judged; has
     vanished;
Those direful heresies of three centuries more,
The hordes barbaric, and, barbaric thrice,
Those Christian Emperors vexing still Christ's Church.
The Antipopes are gone; the Arabian prophet
Scowls at the West in vain.  Yet who can tell
If in some age, remote or near, a cloud
Blacker than aught that shook the olden world
May rush not from clear skies?  That hour upon us,
"Quieta non movere" may become
Wisdom's sum total: to repress, not spur
Progressive thought, the hour's necessity;
Against their will the truthfullest spirits may cry, —
"Better to wait than launch the bark of knowledge
There when the breakers roar!"

                         Work on and fear not!
Work, and in hope, though sin that hope may cheat;
Work, knowing this, that, when God's lesser gifts
Are mocked by mortals, God into that urn

Which stands for aye gift-laden by His throne
Thrusts deeplier yet His hand, and upward draws,
His last — then chief — of mercies, — Retribution.
Should man, abusing, use this knowledge vast,
Not for relieving of God's suffering poor
But doubling of their burthens; not for peace
But keener sharpening of war's battle-axe,
And fleshlier solace of the idle and rich;
God will to such redouble pain for sin.
Such lot may lie before us.   This is sure, —
That, as colossal Sanctity walks oft
In humblest vales, not less a pigmy race
May strut on mountains.   If from heights of science
Men should look forth o'er worlds on worlds unguessed,
And find therein no witness to their God —
Naught but Man's image chaunting hymns to Man, —
"Great is thy wisdom, Man, and strong thy hand," —
God will repay the madness of that boast
With madness guilty less — a brain imbecile.
Races there live, once sage and brave, that now
Know not to light a fire!   If impious men
Press round Truth's gate with Intellect's fleshlier
      lust —
For what is Godless Intellect but fleshly? —
Sudden a glacial wind shall issue forth,
And strike those vile ones blind!
                              Should that day come,
Let no man cease from hope.   Intensest ill
Breeds good intensest.   For the songs of God
That knowledge, won by bad men, will survive.

If fleets one day should pass the onrushing storm,
That Cross which lights their prow will reach but
    sooner
The lands that sit in night.   If Empires new
Wage war on Faith, each drop of martyr blood
Will sow once more Faith's harvest.   Virgin spirits,
Raised from a child-like to an angel pureness,
Will walk in Chastity's sublimer flame;
God's earthquake shake men to their fitting places, —
True men and false, the sons of light and night,
No more, as now, confused.   God's Church will
    make,
Since, though she errs not, yet her best may err,
For sins of good men dead due expiation;
Then for her second triumph claim as site
A planet's, not an empire's girth.   True kings
Will fence their thrones with freemen, not with serfs;
True priests, by serving, rule.   The Tree of Life
First made our spirits food; that Tree which slew us
Will prove her sister.   Knowledge *then* will clasp
Supremacy o'er matter, earth's fruition,
Not by the plucking of a fruit forbidden,
But by the valorous exercise austere
Of faculties, God's gift.   "Lift up your heads,
Ye everlasting gates," the Psalmist sang,
"So shall the King of Glory enter in."
Lives there who doubts that when the Starry Gates
Lift up their heads, like minster porches vast
At feasts before a marvelling nation's eyes,
And show, beyond, the universe of God, —

Lives there who doubts that, entering there, man's
    mind
Must see, before it far, a God who enters,
Flashing from star to star?  Lives there who doubts
That those new heavens, beyond all hope distent,
Must sound their Maker's praise?  Religion's self
That day shall wear an ampler crown; all Truths,—
Now constellated in the Church's Creed,
 Yet dim this day because man's mind is dim,—
Perforce dilating, as man's mind dilates,
O'er us must hang, a new Theology,
Our own, yet nobler,— even as midnight heavens,
Through crystal ether kenned, more sharply shine
Than when mist veiled the stars!  Let others doubt —
My choice is made.

          The stars!  Once more they greet me!
Thanks to the wind that blows yon casement back!
'Tis cold; but vigils old have taught me patience.
Is this the last time, O ye stars?  Not so —
'Tis not the death-chill yet.  Those Northern heavens
Yield me once more that Northern Sign long loved;
Yon sea is still its glass, though many a star
Faints now in broader beams.  Yon winter moon
Has changed this cell, thick-walled and ofttimes
    dim,
Into a silver tent.  O light, light, light,
How great thou art!  Thou only, free of space,
Bindest the universe of God in one.
Matter, methinks, in thee is changed to spirit: —

What if our bodies, death subdued, shall rise
All light — compact of light!
                          I had forgotten
Good Cardinal Schomberg's missive; here it lies;
I read it three weeks since.  "The Holy Father
Wills that your labours stand divulged to Man;
Wills likewise that his name should grace your tome
As dedicate to him."   I read in haste;
That such high grace should 'scape my memory thus
Argues, I think, some failure of my powers.
So be it!  Their task is wrought.
                          The tide descends;
The caves send forth anew those hoarse sea-thunders,
Lulled when full flood satiates their echoing roofs.
They tell me this, that God, their God, hath spoken,
And the great deep obeys.   That deep forsakes
The happy coasts where fishers spread their nets,
The fair green slopes with snowy flocks bespread,
The hamlets, red each morn with cloaks of girls,
And loud with shouting children.   Forth he fares
To solitudes of ocean, waste and wide,
Cheered by that light he loves.   I, too, obey.
I, too, am called to face the Infinite,
Leaving familiar things and faces dear
Of friends and tomes forth leaning from yon wall;
Me, too, the Uncreated Light shall greet,
When cleansed to bear it.   O, how sweet was life!
How sweeter must have been, had I been worthy! —
Grant me Thy Beatific Vision, Lord:
Then shall those eyes, star-wearied, see and live!

# THE YEAR OF SORROW; IRELAND, 1849

## SPRING

ONCE more, through God's high will, and grace
    Of hours that each its task fulfils,
Heart-healing Spring resumes her place,
    The valley throngs, and scales the hills.

In vain.   From earth's deep heart, o'ercharged,
    The exulting life runs o'er in flowers.
The slave unfed is unenlarged;
    In darkness sleep a Nation's powers.

Who knows not Spring?   Who doubts, when blows
    Her breath, that Spring is come indeed?
The swallow doubts not; nor the rose
    That stirs, but wakes not; nor the weed

I feel her near, but see her not;
    For these with pain uplifted eyes
Fall back repulsed, and vapours blot
    The vision of the earth and skies.

I see her not; I feel her near,
    As, charioted in mildest airs,
She sails through yon empyreal sphere,
    And in her arms and bosom bears

That urn of flowers and lustral dews
  Whose sacred balm, o'er all things shed,
Revives the weak, the old renews,
  And crowns with votive wreaths the dead.


Once more the cuckoo's call I hear;
  I know, in many a glen profound,
The earliest violets of the year
  Rise up like water from the ground.


The thorn, I know, once more is white;
  And, far down many a forest dale,
The anemones in dubious light
  Are trembling like a bridal veil.


By streams released, that singing flow
  From craggy shelf through sylvan glades,
The pale narcissus, well I know,
  Smiles hour by hour on greener shades.


The honeyed cowslip tufts once more
  The golden slopes; with gradual ray
The primrose stars the rock, and o'er
  The wood-path strews its milky way.


From ruined huts and holes come forth
  Old men, and look upon the sky!
The Power Divine is on the earth:
  Give thanks to God before ye die!

And ye, O children, worn and weak,
   Who care no more with flowers to play,
Lean on the grass your cold, thin cheek,
   And those slight hands, and, whispering, say,—

"Stern Mother of a race unblest,
   In promise kindly, cold in deed,—
Take back, O Earth, into thy breast,
   The children whom thou wilt not feed."

### SUMMER

Approved by works of love and might,
   The Year, consummated and crowned,
Hath scaled the zenith's purple height,
   And flings his robe the earth around.

Impassioned stillness, fervours calm,
   Brood, vast and bright, o'er land and deep;
The warrior sleeps beneath the palm;
   The dark-eyed captive guards his sleep.

The Iberian labourer rests from toil;
   Sicilian virgins twine the dance;
Laugh Tuscan vales in wine and oil;
   Fresh laurels flash from brows of France.

Far off, in regions of the North,
   The hunter drops his winter fur;
Sun-wakened babes their feet stretch forth;
   And nested dormice feebly stir.

But thou, O land of many woes!
   What cheer is thine?   Again the breath
Of proved Destruction o'er thee blows,
   And sentenced fields grow black in death.


In horror of a new despair
   His blood-shot eyes the peasant strains,
With hands clenched fast, and lifted hair,
   Along the daily darkening plains.


"Why trusted he to them his store?
   Why feared he not the scourge to come?"
Fool! turn the page of History o'er —
   The roll of Statutes — and be dumb!


Behold, O People! thou shalt die!
   What art thou better than thy sires?
The hunted deer a weeping eye
   Turns on his birthplace, and expires.


Lo! as the closing of a book,
   Or statue from its base o'erthrown,
Or blasted wood, or dried-up brook, —
   Name, race, and nation, thou art gone!


The stranger shall thy hearth possess;
   The stranger build upon thy grave!
But know this also — he, not less,
   His limit and his term shall have.

Once more thy volume, open cast,
   In thunder forth shall sound thy name;
Thy forest, hot at heart, at last
   God's breath shall kindle into flame.

Thy brook, dried up, a cloud shall rise,
   And stretch an hourly widening hand,
In God's good vengeance, through the skies,
   And onward o'er the Invader's land.

Of thine, one day, a remnant left
   Shall raise o'er earth a Prophet's rod,
And teach the coasts, of Faith bereft,
   The names of Ireland, and of God.


AUTUMN

Then die, thou Year — thy work is done;
   The work, ill done, is done at last;
Far off, beyond that sinking sun,
   Which sets in blood, I hear the blast

That sings thy dirge, and says, — "Ascend,
   And answer make amid thy peers,
Since all things here must have an end,
   Thou latest of the famine years!"

I join that voice. No joy have I
   In all thy purple and thy gold;
Nor in that nine-fold harmony
   From forest on to forest rolled:

Nor in that stormy western fire
  Which burns on ocean's gloomy bed,
And hurls, as from a funeral pyre,
  A glare that strikes the mountain's head;


And writes on low-hung clouds its lines
  Of ciphered flame, with hurrying hand;
And flings, amid the topmost pines
  That crown the cliff, a burning brand.


Make answer, Year, for all thy dead,
  Who found not rest in hallowed earth;
The widowed wife, the father fled,
  The babe, age-stricken from his birth!


Make answer, Year, for virtue lost;
  For courage, proof 'gainst fraud and force,
Now waning like a noontide ghost;
  Affections, poisoned at their source!


The labourer spurned his lying spade;
  The yeoman spurned his useless plough;
The pauper spurned the unwholesome aid
  Obtruded once, exhausted now.


The roof-trees fall of hut and hall;
  I hear them fall, and falling cry, —
"One fate for each, one fate for all!
  So wills the Law that willed a lie."

Dread power of Man! what spread the waste
   In circles hour by hour more wide,
And would not let the past be past? —
   That Law which promised much, and lied.

Dread power of God, Whom mortal years
   Nor touch, nor tempt, Who sitt'st sublime
In night of night, — O, bid thy spheres
   Resound, at last, a funeral chime!

Call up at last the afflicted race,
   Whom Man, not God, abolished.   Sore,
For centuries, their strife: the place
   That knew them once, shall know no more!


### WINTER

Fall, snow, and cease not!   Flake by flake
   The decent winding-sheet compose;
Thy task is just and pious; make
   An end of blasphemies and woes!

Fall, flake by flake! by thee alone,
   Last friend, the sleeping draught is given;
Kind nurse, by thee the couch is strewn,
   The couch whose covering is from Heaven!

Descend and clasp the mountain's crest;
   Inherit plain and valley deep!
This night, on thy maternal breast,
   A vanquished nation dies in sleep.

Q

Lo! from the starry Temple Gates
 Death rides, and bears the flag of peace;
The combatants he separates;
 He bids the wrath of ages cease.


Descend, benignant Power! But, O,
 Ye torrents, shake no more the vale!
Dark streams, in silence seaward flow!
 Thou rising storm, remit thy wail!


Shake not, to-night, the cliffs of Moher,
 Nor Brandon's base, rough sea! Thou Isle,
The Rite proceeds! From shore to shore,
 Hold in thy gathered breath the while!


Fall, snow! in stillness fall, like dew,
 On church's roof and cedar's fan;
And mould thyself on pine and yew;
 And on the awful face of Man.


Without a sound, without a stir,
 In streets and wolds, on rock and mound,
O omnipresent Comforter,
 By thee, this night, the lost are found!


On quaking moor and mountain moss,
 With eyes upstaring at the sky,
And arms extended like a cross,
 The long-expectant sufferers lie.

Bend o'er them, white-robed Acolyte!
   Put forth thine hand from cloud and mist;
And minister the last sad Rite,
   Where altar there is none, nor priest!

Touch thou the gates of soul and sense;
   Touch darkening eyes and dying ears;
Touch stiffening hands and feet, and thence
   Remove the trace of sins and tears!

And, ere thou seal those filmèd eyes,
   Into God's urn thy fingers dip,
And lay, 'mid eucharistic sighs,
   The sacred wafer on the lip!

This night the Absolver issues forth;
   This night the Eternal Victim bleeds.
O winds and woods, O heaven and earth,
   Be still this night! The Rite proceeds!

# THE SISTERS; OR, WEAL IN WOE

FROM nine to twelve my guest was eloquent
In anger, mixed with sorrow, at the things
He saw around us; lands half marsh, half weeds,
Gates from the gate-posts miserably divorced,
Hovels ill-thatched, wild fences, fissured roads —
"Your people never for the future plan;
They live but for the moment." Thus he spake,
A youth just entering on his broad domains,
A senator in prorogation time
Travelling for knowledge, Oxford's accurate scholar,
A perfect rider, clean in all his ways,
But by traditions narrowed. As the moon
Turns but one side to earth, so showed that world
Whereon he gazed, for stubborn was his will,
And Ireland he had never loved. "You err,"
I answered, taking in good part his wrath,
"Our peasant, too, has prescience; far he sees;
Earth is his foreground only; rough or smooth,
In him from seriousness the lightness comes.
Too serious is he to make sacrifice
For fleeting good; the battles of this world
He with his left hand fights, and half in sport;
He has his moment — and eternity."
"Ay, ay," exclaimed my guest, "your Church, she
    does it!
Your feasts and fasts and wakes and social rites,

With 'Sir,' and 'Ma'am,' and usages of Court.
I've seen a hundred men leave plough and spade
To take a three weeks' infant to its grave,
A cripple pay two shillings for a cart
To bear him to the Holy Well.   Sick Land !
Look up ! the proof is round you written large !
Your Faith is in the balance wanting found.
Your shipless seas confess it ; bridgeless streams ;
Your wasted wealth of ore, and moor, and bay !
Beneath the Upas shade of Faith depraved
All things lie dead — wealth, comfort, freedom, power —
All that great Nations boast !"   "Such things," I
    answered,
"The Gentiles seek ; and you new tests have found ;
' Ecclesiæ stantis vel cadentis,' friend,
' Blessed the rich : blessed whom all men praise ! '
New Scriptures, these ; the Irish keep the old !
Say, are there not diversities of gifts?
Are there not virtues — Industry is one —
Which reap on earth, whilst others sow for heaven ?
Faith, hope, and love, and purity, and patience,
Humility, and self-forgetfulness, —
These too are virtues ; yet they rear not States.
What then?   Of many Nations earth is made ;
Each hath its function ; each its part for others.
If all were hand, where then were ear or eye ?
If all were foot, where head?   You rail, my friend,
Not at my country only, but your own.
The land that gave us birth our service claims,
The suffering land our love.   Yet England, too,

They love, and they the most, who flatter not.
A thousand years of nobleness she lived,
Whereof you rob her!　In this isle are men
By ancient lineage hers.　Such men might say, —
' My England was entombed ere yours had birth.'
Dates she from Arkwright only?　Rose the Nation
With Alfred, or those Tudor Kings who built
The Golden Gate of England's modern time,
But built it upon liberties annulled,
Old glories quenched, the old nobles dead or quelled —
Ay, wrecks more sad?"　His host, I could not use
Words rough as his, albeit to shield a land
For every shaft a targe ; so changed the theme
To her he knew — thence loved.

　　　　　　　　　　　He loved his country ;
An older man than he for things less great
Had loved that land.　Yet who could gaze, unmoved,
From Windsor's terraced heights o'er those broad meads,
Lit by the pomp of silver-winding Thames
Dropping past templed grove, and hall, and farm,
Toward the great City?　Who, unthrilled, could mark
Her Minsters, towering far away, with heads
That stay the sunset of old times ; or them,
Oxford and Cambridge, England's anchors twain,
That to her moorings hold her?　Fresh from these,
Who, who could tread, O Wye, thy watery vale
Where Tintern reigns in ruin ; who could rest
Where Bolton finds in Wharf a warbling choir,
Or where the sea-wind fans thy brow discrowned,

Furness, nor love and wonder? Who, untouched,
When evening creeps from Scawfell toward Black
    Combe,
Could wander by thy darkly gleaming lakes,
Embayed 'mid sylvan garniture and isles
From saint or anchoret named, within the embrace
Of rural mountains green, or sound, scent, touch,
Of kine-besprinkled, soft, partitioned vales,
Almost domestic? Shadow-haunted land!
By Southey's lake Saint Herbert holds his own!
The knightly armour, now, by Yew-dale's crag
Rings loud no longer; Grasmere's reddening glass
Reflects no more the onrushing clan; yet, still,
Thy Saxon Kings, and ever-virgin Queens,
Possess thee with a quiet pathos; still,
Like tarnished path forlorn of moon that sets
Over wide-watered moor and marsh, thy Past
A spiritual sceptre, though deposed, extends
From sea to sea — from century-worn St. Bees
To Cuthbert's tomb under those eastern towers
On Durham's bowery steep!
                    He loved his country;
That love I honoured. Great and strong he called her;
But well I knew that had her greatness waned,
His love had waxed.
              As thus we talked, the sun
Launched through the hurrying clouds a rainy beam
That smote the hills. My guest exclaimed, — "Come
    forth;
We waste the day! Yon ridge my fancy takes;

Climb we its crest!" The wolf-hound at our feet,
Our drift divining, bounded sudden on us,
In rapture of prospective gratitude.

We passed the offending gate; a plank for bridge,
We passed the offending stream, which dashed its spray
Contemptuous on us, proud of liberty.
I laughed: "Our passionate Ireland is the stream;
Seven hundred years at will it mocks or chides;
You have not made it turn your English mill!"
We scaled the hills; we pushed through miles of trees,
Which, sire and son, had held their own since first
The tall elk trod their ways.    Lightning and storm
Had left large wrecks; election wars, not less,
Or hospitalities as fierce, when home
A thousand chiefless clansmen dragged the bride,
Or danced around a cradle,—ah, brave hearts!
Loyal, where cause for loyalty was scant!
Vast were those woods and fair; rock, oak, and yew,
Grey, green, and black, in varying measures striking
That three-stringed lyre which charms not ear but
    eye.                                        .
Long climbing, from the woodland we emerged,
And paced a rocky neck of pale green pasture,
The limit of two counties.    Full in face
Rushed, ocean-scented, the harmonic wind;
Round us the sheep-bells chimed; a shower, late past,
With jewelry had hung the blackberry bush,
And gorse-brake half in gold.    On either side,
Thin-skinned, ascetic, slippery, the descent

Down slanted toward the creeping mists.   Our goal
We reached at last — a broad and rocky mass
Forth leaning, lordly, unto lands remote, —
The lion's head of all those feebler hills
That, cowering, slunk behind it.   Far around,
Low down, subjected, stretched the sea-like waste
Shade-swept, unbounded, like infinity.
An hour before his time the sun had dropped
Behind a mountain-wall of barrier cloud
Wide as the world; but five great beams converged
Toward the invisible seat of his eclipse;
And over many a river, bay, and mere
Lay the dull red of ante-dated eve.

   That summit was a churchyard.   Cross-engraven,
Thronged the close tomb-stones.   Each one prayed
     for peace;
And some were raised by men, whose heads were
     white
Ere selfless toil had won the hoarded coins
That honoured thus a parent.   In the midst,
A tomb-like chapel, thirty feet by ten,
Stood monumental, with stone roof and walls
The wrestling centuries slid from.   Nigh we sat,
While, by the polished angle split, the wind
Hissed like a forkèd serpent.   Silent long
My friend remained; his sallies all had ceased, —
A man of tender nerve though stubborn thought.
The scene weighed on him like a Prophet's scroll
Troubling some unjust City.   Far and near

He scanned the desolate region, and at last
Prayed me the hieroglyphic to expound.
"Yon tower, which blurs the lonely lake far off,
What is it?"   And I answered, — "Know you not?
He built it, he, that Norman horsed and mailed,
Who, strong in Henry's might and Adrian's bull,
Rent from the Gaelic monarch half his realm; —
The rest came later, dowry of the bride."

  Once more he mused;  then, westward pointing,
    spake:
"Yon lovely hills, yet low, with Phidian line,
That melt into the horizon: — on their curve
A ruined castle stands; the sky glares through it,
Red, like a conflagration?"   I replied:
"Four hundred years the Norman held his own;
He spake the people's language; they, in turn,
His war-cry had resounded far and wide;
Their history he had grown, impersonate.
The land rejoiced in him, and of his greatness
Uplifted, glorying, on a neck high held,
The beautiful burden, as the wild stag lifts
O'er rocky Torc his antlers!   Would you more?
The Desmond was unloved beside the Thames;
The right of the great Palatine was trampled;
His Faith by law proscribed.   O'er tombs defaced,
In old Askeaton's Abbey, of his sires,
He vowed unwilling war.   Long years the realm
Reeled like a drunken man.   Behold the end!
Yon wreck speaks all!"

Thus question after question
Dragged, maimed and mangled, dragged reluctant
    forth,
Time's dread confession!  Crime replied to crime;
Whom Tudor planted Cromwell rooted out;
For Charles they fought; — to fight for Kings, their
    spoilers,
The rebel named rebellion!  William next!
Once more the Nobles were down hurled; once more
Nobility as in commission placed
By God among the lowly.  Loyalty
To native Princes, or to Norman chiefs,
Their lawless conquerors, or to British Kings,
Or her, the Mother Church that ne'er betrayed,
Had met the same reward.  The legend spake
Words few but plain, grim rubric traced in blood;
While, like a Fury fleeting through the air,
History from all the octaves of her lyre
Struck but one note!  What rifted tower and keep
Witnessed of tyrannous and relentless wars, —
That, shipless gulfs, that, bridgeless streams and
    moors
Black as if lightning-scarred or curst of God,
Proclaimed of laws blacker than brand or blight —
Those Penal Laws.  The tale was none of mine;
Stone railed at stone; grey ruins dumbly frowned
Defiance, and the ruin-handled blast
Scattered the fragments of Cassandra's curse
From the far mountains to the tombs close by,
Which muttered treason.

                        That sad scene to me
Had lost by use its pathos, as the scent,
Which thrills us while we pass the garden, palls
On one within it tarrying.   To my friend
It spake its natural language; and, as he
Who, hard through habit, reads with voice unmoved
A ballad that once touched him, if perchance
Some listener weeps, partakes that listener's trouble, —
Even so the stranger's sorrow struck on mine,
And I believed the things which I beheld,
There sitting silent.   When at last he spake
The spirit of the man in part was changed;
The things but heard of he had seen; the truths,
Coldly conceded, now he realised;
Justice, at last, with terrible recoil,
Leaped up full-armed, a strong man after sleep,
And dashed itself against the wrong!   I answered:
" Once more you speak the words you spake this morn, —
'Look up, the proof is round you, written large: '
But in an altered sense."


                       I spake, and left him;
Left him to seek a tomb, which three long years
Holds one I honoured.   Half an hour went by;
Then he rejoined me.   With a knitted brow,
And clear vindictiveness of speech, like him
Who, loving, hates the sin of whom he loves,
He spake against the men who, having won
By right or wrong the mastery of this isle
(For in our annals he was versed, nor ran

In custom's blinkers save on modern roads)
Could make of it, seven hundred years gone by,
No more than this! Then I: "No country loved
    they:
Her least, the imperial realm! 'Tis late to mourn;
Let past be past." "The Past," he said, "is present;
And o'er the Future stretches far a hand
Shadowy and minatory." "Come what may,"
I said, "no suffering can to us be new;
No shadow fail to dew some soul with grace.
The history of a Soul holds in it more
Than doth a Nation's! In its every chance
Eternity lies hid; from every step
Branch forth two paths piercing infinity.
These things look noblest from their spiritual side.
A statesman, on the secular side you see them,
And doubt a future based on such a past.
'Tis true, with wrong dies not the effect of wrong,
Or sense thereof; 'tis true, stern Power with time
Changes its modes, not instinct; true it is,
That hollow peace is war that wears a mask;
Yet, let us quell to-day unquiet thoughts.
She rests who lies in yonder tomb; sore pains
She suffered; yet within her there was peace;
In God's high Will she rests, and why not we?"

Thus we conversed till twilight, thickening, crept,
Compassionate, o'er a scene to which, we said,
Twilight seemed native, day a garish vest
Worn by a slave. Returning, oft my friend

Cast loose in wrath the arch-rebel, Truth; I answered:
"She rests, and why not we? O suffering land!
Thee, too, God shields; and only for this cause
Can they that love thee sleep." —
Holy were all as she, the wrongs long past
Would rack our age no longer; for that cause,
The blinder they who mock her country's Faith.
Thousands are like her! Ireland's undergrowths —
Her hope is there, and not in cloud or sunshine
That beat her mountain-tops. The maiden's tale
He sought with instance. 'Twas not marvellous,
I told him; yet, to calm his thoughts perturbed,
Thus, while the broad moon o'er the lonely moor
Rose, blanching as she soared, till pools, at first
With trembling light o'erlaid, gave back her face,
And all the woodland waves, as eve advanced,
Shone bright o'er sombre hollows, I recounted
The fragments of a noteless Irish life,
Not strange esteemed among us. Such a theme
I sought not. Ill it were to forge for friend
A providence, or snare him, though to Truth.
Yet I was pleased he sought that tale. 'Twas sad;
But in its dusky glass — and this I hid not —
Shadowed a phantom image of my country,
Vanquished yet victor, in her weal and woe.

### THE TALE

The father in the prime of manhood died;
The mother followed soon; their children twain,
Margaret Mac Carthy, and her sister Mary,

The eldest scarcely ten years old, survived
To spread cold hands upon a close-sealed grave,
And cry to those who answered not.   The man,
Who, in that narrow spot to them the world,
Stood up and seemed as God; that gentler one,
Who overhung like Heaven their earliest thought,
And in the bosom of whose sleepless love
Re-born they seemed each  morning, — both  were
    dead.
In grief's bewilderment the orphans stood,
Like one by fraud betrayed; nor moon, nor sun,
Nor trees, nor grass, nor herds, nor hills appeared
To them what they had been.   In saddened eyes,
Frightened yet dull, in voice subdued, and feet
That moved as though they feared to wake the dead,
Men saw that nowhere loneliness more lives
Than in the breasts of children.   Time went by;
The farm was lost; and to her own small home
Their father's mother led them.   'Twas not far;
They could behold the orchard they had loved;
Behind the hedge could hear the robin sing,
And the bees murmur.   Slowly, as the trance
Of grief dissolved, the present lived once more;
The past became a dream!

                       I see them still!
Softly the beauty-making years on went,
And each one, as he passed our planet's verge,
Looked back, and left a gift.   A darker shade
Dropped on the deepening hair; a brighter gleam
Forth flashed from sea-blue eyes with darkness fringed.

Like, each to each, their stature growing kept
Unchanged gradation.    To her grandmother
A quick eye and a serviceable hand
Endeared the elder most; she kept the house;
Hers was the rosier cheek, the livelier mind,
The smile of readier cheer.    In Mary lived
A visionary and pathetic grace,
Through all her form diffused, from those small feet
Up to that beauteous-shaped and netted head,
Which, from the slender shoulders and slight bust,
Rose like a queen's.    Alone, not solitary,
Full often half an autumn day she sat
On the high grass-banks, foot with foot enclasped,
Now twisting osiers, watching cloud-shades now,
Or rushing vapours through whose chasms there shone,
Far off, an alien race of clouds, like Alps
O'er Courmayeur white-gleaming, and like them
To stillness frozen.    Well that orphan knew them,
Those marvellous clouds that roof our Irish wastes;
Spring's lightsome veil outblown, sad Autumn's bier,
And Winter's pillar of electric light
Slanted from heaven.    A spirit-world, so seemed it,
In them was imaged forth to her.

                                        With us
The childish heart betroths itself full oft
In vehement friendship.    Mary's was of these;
And thus her fancy found that counterweight
Which kept her feet on earth.    With her there walked
Two years a little maiden of the place,
Her comrade, as men called her.    Eve by eve,

Homeward from school we saw them as they passed,
One arm of each about the other's neck,
Above both heads a single cloak.   She died,
To Mary leaving what she valued most,
A rosary strung with beads from Olivet.
Daily did Mary count those beads; from each
The picture of some Christian Truth ascending,
Till all the radiant Mysteries shone on high
Like constellations, and man's gloomy life
For her to music rolled on poles of love
Through realms of glory.   Hope makes Love immortal!
That friend she ne'er forgot.   In later years
Working with other maidens equal-aged,
(A lady of the land instructed them)
In circle on the grass, not them she saw,
Heard not the song they sang; alone she sat,
And heard, 'mid sighing pines and murmuring streams,
The voice of the departed.
                                   Smoothly flowed,
Till Margaret had attained her eighteenth year,
The tenor of their lives; and they became,
Those sisters twain, a name in all the vale
For beauty, kindness, truth, for modest grace,
And all that makes that fairest flower of all
Earth bears, heaven fosters — peasant nobleness: —
For industry the elder.   Mary failed
In this, a dreamer; indolence her fault,
And self-indulgence, — not that coarser sort
Which seeks delight, but that which shuns annoy.
And yet she did her best.   The dull red morn

R

Shone, beamless, through the wintry hedge while
    passed
That pair with panniers, or, on whitest brows
The balanced milk-pails.   Margaret ruled serene
A wire-fenced empire smiling through soft glooms,—
The pure, health-breathing dairy.   Softer hand
Than Mary's ne'er let loose the wool; no eye
Finer pursued the on-flowing line; her wheel
Murmured complacent joy, like kitten pleased;
With us such days abide not.
                  Sudden fell
Famine, the Terror never absent long,
Upon our land.   It shrank — the daily dole;
The oatmeal trickled from a tighter grasp;
Hunger grew wild through panic; infant cries
Maddened at times the gentle into wrong;
Death's gentleness more oft for death made way;
And, like a lamb that openeth not its mouth,   ·
The sacrificial People, fillet-bound,
Stood up to die.   Amid inviolate herds
Not few the sacraments of death received,—
Then waited God's decree.   These things are known;
Strangers have witnessed to them; strangers writ
The epitaph again and yet again;
The nettles and the weeds by the way-side
Men ate; from sharpening features and sunk eyes
Hunger glared forth, a wolf more lean each hour;
Children seemed pigmies shrivelled to sudden age;
And the deserted babe, too weak to wail,
But shook if hands, pitying or curious, raised

The rag across him thrown.   In England, alms
From many a private hearth were largely sent,
As ofttimes they have been.   'Twas vain.   The land
Wept, while her sons sank back into her graves
Like drowners 'mid still seas.   Who could, escaped;
And, on a ghost-thronged deck, amid such cries
As from the battle-field ascend at night,
When stumbling widows grope o'er heaps of slain,—
Amid such cries stood Mary, when the ship
Its cable slipped, and, on the populous quays
Grating, without a wind, on the slow tide,
Dropped downward to the main.

                              For western shores
Those emigrants were bound.   At Liverpool,
Fanned by the ocean breeze the smouldering fire
Of fever burst into a sudden flame;
The stricken there were left; among them Mary.
How long she knew not, in an hospital,
A Babel of confused distress, she lay,
Dinned with delirious strife.   But o'er her brow
God shook the dew of dreams wherein she trod
The shadowed wood-walks of old days once more,
And dabbled in old streams.   Ere long, still weak,
Abroad she roamed, a basket on her arm,
With violets heaped.   The watchman of the city
Laid his strong hand upon her drooping head,
Banning the impostor.   'Twas her rags, she thought,
Incensed him, and in meekness moved she on.
When one, with lubrique smile, toyed with her flowers,
And spake of violet eyes and easier life,

She understood not, but misliked, and passed.
In Liverpool an agèd priest she found,
A kinsman of her mother's.   Much to her
Of emigrants he spake, and of their trials —
Old ties annulled—and 'mid temptations strange
Lacking full oft the Bread of Life.   She wept;
Before the tabernacle's lamp she prayed
Freshly-absolved and heavenliest, with a prayer
That showered God's blessing o'er the wanderers
       down;
But dead was her desire to cross the main.
Her strength restored, beyond the city-bound
With others of her nation she abode,
Amid the gardens labouring.   A rough clan
Those outcasts seemed; not like their race at home;
Nor chapel theirs, nor school.   Their strength was
       prized;
Themselves were so esteemed as that sad tribe
Beside the Babylonian streams that wept,
By those that loved not Sion.
                              Weeks grew months;
And, with the strength to suffer, sorrow came.
Hard by their nomad camp, a youth there lived
Of wealthier sort, who looked upon this maid.
Her country was his own; he loved it not;
Had rooted quickly in the stranger's land;
And, versatile, cordial, specious, seeming-frank,
Contracting for himself a separate peace,
Had prospered, but had prospered in such sort
As they that starve within.   Her confidence

He gained.   To love unworthy, still he loved her;
Loved with the love of an unloving heart,—
That love which either is in shallows lost,
Or in its black depth breeds the poison weed.
She knew him not; how could she?   He himself
Knew scantly.   Near her, what was best within him
Her golden smile sunned forth; but, dark and cold,
Like a benighted hemisphere, abode
A moiety of his being, which she saw not.
His was a superficial nature, vain,
And hard, to good impressions sensitive,
And most admiring virtues least his own;
A mirror that took in a seeming world,
And yet remained blank surface.   He was crafty,
Followed the plough with diplomatic heart;
His acts were still like the knight's move at chess,
Each a surprise; not less, to nature's self
Who heard him still referred them.   "What!" men
     said,—
"Marry the portionless!"   Strange are fortune's
     freaks!
The wedding-day was fixed, the ring brought home,
When from a distant uncle tidings came:
His latest son was dead.   "Take thou my farm,
And share my house "— so spake the stern old man —
"And wed the wife whom I for thee have found."
He showed the maid that letter.   Slowly the weeds
Made way adown the thick and stifled stream,
And others followed; slowly sailed the cloud
Through the dull sky, and others followed slowly;

At last he spake.   Low were his words and thin,
Many, but scarcely heard.   He asked — her counsel!
Her cheek one moment burned.   Death-cold, once
    more,
A little while she sat; then rose and said:
"You would be free; I free you; go in peace."
'Twas the good angel in his heart that loved her;
'Twas not the man himself!   He wept, but went.
The woman of the house that night was sure
The girl had loved him not.   She thought not so,
When, four months past, she marked her mouth, aside,
Tremble, his name but uttered.

                              Sharp the wrong!
Yet they on Life's bewildered book would force
A partial gloss it bears not, who assume
The injured wholly free from blame.   The world
Is not a board in squares of black and white,
Or else the judgment-executing tongue
Would lack probation.   Wronged men are not angels;
Wrong's chiefest sin is this — it genders wrong;
So stands the offender in his own esteem
Exculpate, while the feebly-judging starve
The just cause, babbling "mutual was the offence!"
The man was weak; not wholly vile.   'Twas well,
Doubtless, to free him; yet in after years,
When early blight had struck his radiant head,
The girl bewailed the pride that left, thus tempted,
The man she loved; arraigned the wrath that left him
Almost without farewell.   His letter, too,
Unopened she returned.   'Twas strange! so sweet —

Not less there lived within her, down, far down,
A fire-spring seldom wakened! When a child,
At times, by some strange jealousy disturbed,
From her still dream she flashed in passion quelled
Ere from her staider sister's large blue eyes
The astonishment had passed. Such moods remained,
Though rare — that wrath of tender hearts, which scorns
Revenge, which scarcely utters its complaint,
And yet forgives but slowly.
                                   In those days,
Within the maiden's bosom, there arose
Sea-longings, and desire to sail away
She knew not whither; and her arms she spread,
Weeping, to winds and waves, and shores unknown,
Lighted by other skies; and inly thus
She reasoned, self-deceived. " What keeps thee here?
'Twas for a farther bourne thou bad'st farewell
To those at home, and here thou art as one
That hangs between two callings." In her heart,
Tempests, low-toned, to ocean-tempests yearned,
And ever, when she marked the shipmast forest
That on the smoky river swayed far off,
Her wish became a craving. Soon, once more,
Alone, 'mid hundreds on a rain-washed deck
She stood, and saw the billows heave around
And all the passions of that headlong world.
Dark-visaged ocean frowned with hoary brows
Against dark skies; huge, lumbering water-weights

Went shouldering through the abysses; streaming
    clouds
Ran on the lower levels of the wind;
And, in the universe of things, she seemed
An atom, random blown.   Full many a morn
Rose red through mists, like babe that weeps to rise;
Full many an evening died from wave to wave;
Then gradual peace possessed her.   Love may wound,
But 'tis self-love that wound exasperates;
A noble nature casts out bitterness,
And o'er the scar, like pine-tree incorrupt,
Weeps healing gums.   Heart-whole she gazed at last
On the great city, chiefest of that realm
Which wears the Future's glory.   Landed, soon
Back to old duties with a mightier zest
Her heart, its weakening sadness passed, returned.
Kindness made service easier, and the tasks,
At first distasteful, smiled on her ere long.
There she was loved once more; there all went well;
And there in peace she might have lived and died.
Yet in that region she abode not long.
In part, a wayward instinct drave her forth;
In part, a will that from the accomplished end,
Unstable, swerved; in part, a hope forlorn.
She sought a site, their sojourn who had left
Long since her village.   There old names, old voices,
Faces unknown, yet recognised, thronged round her
In unconsummate union (hearts still like,
Yet all beside so different), not like Souls
Re-met in heaven — more like those Shades antique

That, 'mid the empurpled fields, of other airs
Mindful, in silence trod the lordly land,
Or flocked around the latest guest of Death
With question sad of home.   Imperfect ties
Rub severance into soreness.   Mary passed,
Thus urged, ere long to lonelier climes; she tracked,
Companioned sometimes, sometimes without friend,
The boundless prairie, sailed the sea-like lake,
Descended the broad river as it rushed
Through immemorial forests; lastly stood
Sole, 'mid that city by the southern sea.
   There sickness fell upon her; there her hand
Dropt, heavier daily, on her task half done;
Her feet wore chains unseen.   The end, she thought,
Was coming.   Ofttimes, in her happier days,
She wished to die, and be with God; yet now,
Wearied by many griefs, to life she clung,
Upbraiding things foregone and inly sighing,—
"None loves to die."   Sorrow, earth-born, in some
Breeds first the Earth-infection; in them works,
Like those pomegranate seeds that barred from light
For aye sad Ceres' child!   Alas! how many,
The ill-honoured ecstasies of youth surceased,
Exchange its clear spring for the mire!   Hope sick,
How oft Faith dies!   How few are they in whom
Virgin but yields to Vestal; casual pureness
Merged in essential; childhood's matin dew
Fixed, ere exhaled, in the Soul's adamant!
Mary with these had part; to her help came —
That help the proud despise.   One eve, it chanced,

Upon the vast and dusking quays she stood,
Alone and weeping.   She that morn had sent
Her latest hoardings to her grandmother,
And half was sorry she had naught retained.
The warm rain wet her hair; she heard, within,
The silver ringing of its drops commingling
With that still mere beside her childhood's home,
And with the tawny sedge that girt it round,
And with its winter dogwood far away
Reddening the faint, still gleam.   As thus she stood,
Upon her shoulder sank a hand.   She turned;
It was a noble lady, clothed in black,
And veiled.   That veil thrown back, she recognised
At once the luminous stillness and the calm
Ethereal which the sacred cloister breeds.
A voice, as pure and sweet as if from heaven,
Toned as friend speaks to friend, addressed her thus:
"You lack a home: our convent is hard by."
    The lady, Spanish half, and Irish half,
No answer sought, but with compulsion soft
Drew her, magnetic, as the tree hard by
Draws the poor creeper on the ground diffused,
And lifts it into light.   The child's cold hand
Lurked soon in hers; and in that home, which seemed
An isle of heaven, the meek lay-sister lived,
Ere long by healthier airs to strength restored,—
A rapturous life of Christian freedom masked
In what but servitude had been to one
Lacking vocation true.   The Life Divine,
"Hidden with God," is hidden from the world,

Lest Virtue should be dimmed by Virtue's praise.
Heroic Virtue least by men is prized.
The hero in the saint the crowd can honour,—
The saint, at best, forgive.   To this world's ken,
Convents, of sanctity chief citadels —
Though sanctity in every place is found —
The snowy banners and bright oriflambs
Of that resplendent realm by Counsels ruled,
Not Precept only, — spread in vain, despised,
Or for their earthly good alone revered,
Not for their claims celestial.   Different far
The lesson Mary learned.   The poor were fed,
The orphan nursed; around the sick man's couch,
Gentle as light, hovered the healing hand;
And beautiful seemed, on mountain-tops of truth,
The foot that brought good tidings!   Times of trial
Were changed to Sabbaths; and the rude, rough girl,
Waiting another service, found a home
Where that which years had marred returned once more,
Like infant flesh clothing the leprous limb.
Yet these things Mary found, were blossoms only;
The tree's deep root was secret.   From the Vow,
Which bound the Will's infinitude to God,
Upwelled that peaceful strength whose fount was God;
From Him, behind His sacramental veil
In holy passion for long hours adored,
Came that great Love, which made the bonds of earth
Needless, thence irksome.   Wondering, there she
    learned
The creature was not for the creature made,

But for the sole Creator; that His kingdom,
Glorious hereafter, lies around us here,
Its visible splendour painfully suppressing,
And waiting its transfigurance.　Was it strange,
If, while those Brides of Christ around her moved,
Her heart sang hymns to God?　Much had she
　　　suffered;
Much of her suffering, gladly there she learned,
Came of her fault; and much had kindliest ends,
Not yet in her fulfilled.　A light o'ershone her,
Which slays Illusion,— that white snake which slimes
The labyrinth of self-love's more tender ways,
Virtue's most specious mimic.　She was loosed;
The actual by the seeming thraldom slain;
Her life was from within and from above;
And, as, when Winter dies and Spring new-born
Her whisper breathes o'er earth, the earlier flowers,
Unlike the wine-dark growths of Autumn dipped
In the year's sunset, rise in lightest hues —
An astral gleam, white, green, or delicate yellow
More light than colour,— so the maiden's thoughts
Flashed with a radiance that permitted scarce
Human affections tragic.　Oft, she told me,
As faithless to old friends she blamed herself : —
One hand touched Calvary, one the Eternal Gates;
The present nothing seemed.　The years passed on;
The honeymoon of this heart-bridal waned;
But nothing of its spousal truth was lost,
Nor of its serious joy.　If failures came —
And much she marvelled at her slow advance,

And for the first time, pierced by that stern grace
Wherein no sin looks trivial, feared; — what then?
Failures, that deepened humbleness, but sank
Foundations deeper for a loftier pile
Of solid virtue; transports, homeward summoned,
For more disinterested love made way,
More perfect made Obedience.
                              If a Soul,
Half-way to heaven, death past, once more to earth
Were sent, it could but feel as Mary felt,
When on the convent grates a letter smote,
Loud, harsh, with summons from the outward world.
Her sister, such its tidings, was a wife,
(That matron whom you praised: — ay, comely is she,
And good; laborious, kindly, faithful, true;
Yet Time has done Time's work, her spiritual beauty
Transposing gently to a lower key),
Her grandmother bereft, and weak through age,
Needed her tendance sorely.   Would she come?
Alas! what could she?   Duty stretched from far
An iron hand that stayed her mounting steps;
The little novices wept aloud, — "Abide!"
Long on her neck the saintly sisterhood
Hung ere they blessed her; then she turned, and went.

    And so once more she trod this rocky vale,
And scarcely older looked at twenty-six
Than at sixteen.   Before so gentle, now
A humbler gentleness was o'er her thrown;
Nor ruffled was she ever, as of yore,

With gusts of flying spleen: nor feared she now
Hindrance unlovely, or the word that jarred.
The sadness, hers at first, dispersed ere long,
And such strange sweetness came to her, men said
A mad dog would not bite her.   Lowliest toils
Were by her hand ennobled; Labour's staff
Beneath it burst in blossom.   In the garden,
'Mid earliest birds, and singing like a bird,
She moved, her grandmother asleep.   She mixed
The reverence, due to years, with tenderness,
The infant's claim.   'Twas hers to bring the crutch,
Nor mark the lameness; hers with question apt
To prompt, not task, the memory.   Tales twice-told
Wearied not her, nor orders each with each
At odds, nor causeless blame.   Wiles she had many
To anticipate harsh moods, lest one rash word
Might draw a cloud 'twixt helpless eld and heaven,
Blotting the Eternal Vision, felt not seen
By hearts in grace.   With works of gay caprice,
Needless — yet prized — she made the spectre, Want,
Seem farther off.   Thus love in narrow space
Built a great world.   The grandmother preferred
To her, that dreamful girl of old, the woman
Who from the mystic precinct first had learned
Humanity, yet seemed a human creature
O'erruled by some angelic guest.   At heart
Ever a nun, she ministered with looks
That healed the sick.   The newly-widowed door
Its gloom remitted when she passed; stern foes
Downtrod their legend of old wrongs.   To her

Sacred were those that grieved; — those, tearless yet,
Sacred scarce less, because they smiled, nor knew
The ambushed fate before them.   When a child,
Grey-haired companionship or solitude
Had pleased her more than childish mates; but, now,
All the long eves of summer in the porch
The children of her sister and the neighbours,
A spotless flock, sat round her.   From her smiles
The sluggish mind caught light, the timid heart
Courage and strength.   Unconscious thus, each day
Her soft and blithesome feet one letter traced
In God's great Book above.   So passed her life; —
Sorrow had o'er it hung a gentle cloud;
But, like an autumn-mocking day in spring,
Dewy and dim yet ending in pure gold,
The sweets were sweeter for the rain, the growth
Stronger for shadow.

                You have seen her tomb!
Upon the young and beautiful it closed:
Her grandmother yet lingers!   What is Time?
Shut out the sun, and all the summer long
The fruit-tree stands as barren as the rock;
May's offering March can bring us.   Of the twain,
The younger, doubtless, in the eyes of God,
Had inly lived the longest.   She had learned
From action much, from suffering more, far more,
For stern Experience is a sword whose point
Makes way for Truth.   Her trials, great and little,
And trials ever keep proportion just
With high vocations and the spirit's growth,

Had done their work till all her inner being,
Freed from asperities, in the light of God
Shone like the feet of some old crucifix
Kissed into smoothness.    Here I fain would end,
Leaving her harboured; but her stern, kind fates
Not thus forewent her.    Like her life her death,
Not negative or neutral; great in pains,
In consolations greater.    Many a week
Much ailed her; what the cause remained in doubt;
When certainty had come, she trembled not;
Fixed was her heart.    Those pangs that shook her
        frame,
Like tempests roaring round a mountain church,
Shook not that peace within her!    She was thankful;
" More pain if such Thy Will, and patience more,"—
This was her prayer; or, wiping from moist eyes
The trembling tear, she whispered, — " Give me, Lord,
On earth Thy cleansing fire that I may see
Sooner Thy Face, death past! "
                              Alleviations,
Many and great, God granted her.    Once more
Her sister was her sister!    Unlike fortunes
Had placed at angles those two lives that once
Lay side by side; and love, that could not die,
Had seemed to sleep.    It woke; and, as from mist,
Once more shone out their childhood!    Laughed and
        flashed
Once more the garden-beds whose bright accost
Had cheered them for their parents mourning.    Tears
Remembered stayed the course of later tears;

The prosperous from the unprosperous sister sought
Heart-peace; nor wealth nor care could part them
    more;
And sometimes Margaret's children seemed to her
As children of another! Greetings sweet
Cheered her from distant regions. Once, it chanced,
The nuns a relic sent her, ne'er before
Seen in our vales, a fragment of that Cross
Whereon the world's Redeemer hung three hours:—
The neighbours entering knelt and wept, and smote
Their breasts; her hands she raised in prayer; and
    straight
Such Love, such Reverence in her heart there rose,
Her anguish, like a fiend exorcised, fled;
And for an hour at peace she lay as one
Imparadised. A solace too was hers,
Known but to babes. Her body, not her mind,
Was racked; the pang to come she little feared,
Nor lengthened out morose the pang foregone;
Once o'er, to sleep she sank in thankful prayer.

    A week ere Mary died all suffering left her;
And, from the realms of glory, beams, as though
Further restraint they brooked not, fell on her
Yet militant below, as there she lay
In monumental whiteness, spirit-lit.
The anthems of her convent charmed once more
Her dreams; and scents from woods where she had sat
In tears. Then spake she of her wandering days;—
Herself she scarcely seemed to see in them;
  s

Plainly thus much I saw: When all went well,
Danger stood nigh; but, soon as sorrow came,
Within that darkness nearer by her side
Walked her good Angel.   In that latest week,
Some treasures hidden ever near her heart
She showed me: faded flowers; her mother's hair;
Gold pieces that have raised our chapel's Cross;
A riband by her youthful comrade worn: —
Upon its cover some few words I found
There traced, when first beyond the western main
She heard the homeless cuckoo's cry well-known:
"When will my People to their land return?"
    From the first hour her grandchild sank, once more
She that for years bed-ridden lay had risen,
And, autumn past, put forth a wintry strength,
Ministering.   Her frame was stronger than her mind;
O'er that at times a dimness hung, like cloud
That creeps from pine to pine.   Inly she missed
Her wonted place of homage lost; she mused
Sadly upon the solitary future;
But in her there abode a rock-like will,
And from her tearless service night or day
No man might push her.   Seldom spake the woman;
She called her grandchild by her daughter's name,
Her daughter buried thirty years and more,
And once she said in wrath, — "Why toil they thus?
Nora is dead."   She laboured till the end.
It came — that mortal close!   'Twas Christmas Eve;
Far, far away were heard the city bells;
The sufferer slept.   At midnight I went forth;

Along the ice-filmed road a dull gleam lay,
And a sepulchral wind in woods far off
Sang dirges deep.  Upon her crutches bent,
The aged woman stood beside the door,
With that long gaze intense, which is an act,
Silently looking toward that hill of graves
We trod to-day; a sinking moon shone o'er it:
Then whispered she — the light of buried years
Edging once more her eyes — " Each Saturday,
Of those that in that churchyard sleep three Souls,
Their penance done, ascend, and are with God."
    Thus as she spake a cry was heard within,
And many voices raised the Litany
For a departing Soul.   Long time — too long —
Had seemed that dying!   Now the hour was come,
And change ineffable announced that Death
At last was standing on the floor.   O hour,
When in brief space our life is lived again!
Down cast the latest stake! when fiends ascend,
Beckoning the phantoms of forgotten sins
Conscience to scare, or launching as from slings
Temptations new; while Angels hold before us
The Cross unshaken as the sun in heaven,
And whisper, — " Christ."   O hour, when prayer is all!
And they that clasp the hand are thrown apart
By the world's breadth from that they love!   The act,
Sin's dread bequest that makes an end of sinning,
Long lasted, while the heart-strings snapt, and all
The elements of the wondrous sensuous world
Slid from the fading sense, and those poor fingers,

As the loose precipice of life down crumbled,
Plucked as at roots.   Storm-winged, the hours rushed
     by;
There lay she like some bark on midnight seas,
Now toiling through the windless vale, anon
Hurled on and up to meet the implacable blast
Upon the rolling ridge, when not a foot
Can tread the decks, and all the sobbing planks
Tremble o'erspent.   The morning dawned at last,
Whitening the frosty pane; the lights removed,
(Save that tall candle in her hand sustained
By others) she descried it: "Ah!" she said,
"Thank God! another day!"   Then, noting one
Who near her knelt, she said,— "The night is sped,
And you have had no sleep; alas! I thought
Ere midnight I should die."   Her eyelids closed;
Into a sleep, as quiet as a babe's,
Gradual she sank; and, while the ascending sun
Shot 'gainst the western hill his earliest beam,
In sleep, without a sigh, her spirit passed.

   I would you could have seen her face in death!
I would you could have heard that last dread rite,
The mighty Mother's, o'er the stormy gulf
And all the moanings of the unknown abyss
Flinging victorious anthems, or the strength
Of piercing prayer: "Oh! ye, at least, my friends,
Have pity on me! plead for me with God!"
That Rite complete, the dark procession wound
Interminably through the fields and farms,
While, wailing like a midnight wind, the *keen*

Expired o'er moor and heath.   At eve we reached
The graveyard; slowly, as to-day, the sun
Behind a tomb-like bank of leaden cloud
Dropt while the coffin sank, and died away
The latest Miserere ——

                    More than once
I would have ceased; but he, my friend and guest,
Or touched or courteous, willed me to proceed.
Perhaps that tale the wild scene harmonised
By sympathy occult; perhaps it touched him,
Contrasting with his recent life — with England,
With Oxford, long his home; its ordered pomp;
Its intermingled groves, and fields, and spires,
Its bridges spanning waters calm and clear;
The frequentation of its courts; its chimes;
Its sunset towers, and strangely youthful gardens
That breathe the ardours of the budding year
On the hoar breadth of grove-like cloisters old,
Chapels, and libraries, and statued halls,
England's still saintly City!   Time has there
A stone tradition built like that all round
Woven by the inviolate hedges, where the bird
Her nest has made and warbled to her young,
May after May secure, since the third Edward
Held his last tournament, and Chaucer sang
To Blanche and to Philippa lays of love —
Not like Iernian records.   Sad we rose,
That tale complete; and, after silence long,
As homeward through the braided forest-skirt

We trod the moonlight-spotted rocks, my friend
Resumed, with pregnant matter, oft more just
In thought than application; but his voice
Was softer than it used to be.   At last,
After our home attained, we turned, and, lo!
With festal fires the hills were lit!   Thine eve,
Saint John, had come once more; and for thy sake,
As though but yesterday thy crown were won,
Amid their ruinous realm uncomforted
The Irish people triumphed.   Gloomy lay
The intermediate space; thence brightlier burned
The circling fires beyond it.   "Lo!" said I,
"Man's life as viewed by Ireland's sons; a vale
With many a pitfall thronged, and shade, and briar,
Yet over-blown by angel-haunted airs,
And by the Light Eternal girdled round."
   Brief supper past, within the porch we sat,
As fire by fire burned low.   We spake; were mute;
Resumed; but our discourse was gently toned,
Touched by a spirit from that wind-beaten grave,
Which breathed among its pauses, as of old
That converse Bede records, when by the sea,
'Twixt Tyne and Wear, facing toward Lindisfarne,
Saxon Ceolfrid and his Irish guest,
Evangelist from old Iona's isle,
'Mid the half Pagan land in cloisters dim
Discussed the Tonsure, and the Paschal time,
Sole themes whereon, in sacred doctrine one,
They differed; but discussed them in such sort
That mutual reverence deeper grew.   We heard

The bridgeless brook that sang far off, and sang
Alone; for not among us builds that bird
Which changes light to music, haply ill-pleased
That Ireland bears not yet, in song's domain,
To Spenser worthy fruit.   Our beds at last,
Wearied, yet glad, we sought.   Ere long the wind,
Gathering its manifold voices and the might
Of all its wills in valleys far, and rolled
From wood to wood o'er ridge and ravine, woke
Those Spectres which o'erhang my sleep in storm, —
A hundred hills to me by sound well known,
That stand dark clustered in the night, and bend
With rainy skirt o'er lake and prone morass,
Or by sea-bays lean out procumbent brows,
Waiting the rising sun.

                         At morn we met
Once more, my friend and I.   The evening's glow
Had from his feelings passed; in their old channels
They flowed, scarce tinged.   But still his thoughts
    retained
The trace of late impressions quaintly linked
With kindred thought-notes earlier.   Half his mind
Scholastic was; his fancy deep; the age
Alone had stamped him modern.   Much he spake
Of England wise and wealthy — now no more,
He said, "a haughty nation proud in arms,"
Nor, as in Saxon times, a crownèd child
Propped 'gainst the Church's knee; but ocean's
    Queen,
Spanning the world with golden zone twin-clasped

By Commerce and by Freedom!   But no less
Of pride and suffering spake he, and that frown
Sun-pressed on brows once pure.   Of Ireland next: —
How strange a race, more apt to fly than walk;
Soaring yet slight; missing the good things round
      them,
Yet ever out of ashes raking gems;
In instincts loyal, yet respecting law
Far less than usage; changeful, yet unchanged!
Timid, yet enterprising; frank, yet secret;
Untruthful oft in speech, yet living truth,
And Truth in things divine to life preferring: —
Scarce men; yet possible angels!   "'Isle of Saints!'
Such doubtless was your land — again it might be —
Strong, prosperous, manly never! ye are Greeks
In intellect, and Hebrews in the soul:
The solid Roman heart, the corporate strength,
Is England's dower!"   "Unequally, if so,"
I said, "in your esteem the Isles are matched.
They live in distant ages, alien climes;
Native they are to diverse elements.
Our swan walks awkwardly upon dry land;
Your boasted strength in spiritual needs so helps you
As armour helps the knight who swims a flood."
He laughed.   "At least no siren streams for us,
Nor holy wells!   We love 'the fat of the land,'
Meads such as Rubens painted!   Strange our fates!
Our feast is still the feast of fox and stork,
The platter broad, and amphora long-necked; —
Ill sorted yoke-mates truly.   Strength, meanwhile,

Lords it o'er weakness!"  "Never yet," I answered,
"Was husband vassal to an intricate wife
But roared he ruled her;" ere his smile had ceased,
Continuing thus: "Ay! strength o'er weakness
    rules!
Strength hath in this no choice.  But what is Strength?
Two Strengths there are.  Club-lifting Hercules,
A mountained mass of gnarled and knotted sinews,
How shows he near the intense, Phœbean Might
That, godlike, spurns the ostent of thews o'ergrown;
That sees far off the victory fixed and sure,
And, without effort, wings the divine death
Like light, into the Python's heart?  My friend,
Justice is strength; union on justice built;
Good-will is strength — kind words — silence — that
    truth
Which hurls no random charge.  Your scribes long
    time
Blow on our island like a scythèd wind;
The good they see not, nor the cause of ill;
They tear the bandage from the wound half-healed.
Is not such onset weakness?  Were it better,
Tell me, free-trader staunch, for sister Nations
To make exchange for aye of scorn for scorn,
Or blend the nobler powers and aims of each,
Diverse, and for that cause correlative,
True commerce, noblest, holiest, frankest, best,
And breed at last some destiny to God
Glorious, and kind to man? — If torn apart
One must her empire lose, and one her all."

Thus as we spake, the hall clock vast and old,
A waif from Spain's Armada, chimed eleven;
And from the stables drew a long-haired boy
Who led a horse as shaggy as a dog,
A splenetic child of thistles and hill blast,
Rock-ribbed, and rich in craft of every race
From weasel to the beast that feigns to die.
Mounting — alas, that friends should ever part! —
My guest bade thus adieu: "For good or ill
Our lands are linked."   And I rejoined, "For which?
This shall you answer, when, your pledge fulfilled,
Before the swallow you return, and meet
The unblown Spring in our barbaric vale."

# LYRICS, SONNETS, AND EPIGRAMS

Not willingly the Muses sing of love;
　But, ere their Songs disperse o'er man's domain,
　Through the dark chambers of the poet's brain
They pass, and passing take the stamp thereof;
And, as the wind that sweeps the linden grove
　Wafts far its odour, so that sphere-born Strain
　Learns from its mortal mould to mourn and plain,
Though the strong Muses sit like Gods above.

True poetry is doubly-dowered — a brightness,
　Lit from above, yet fuelled from below;
　A moon that rolls through heaven in vestal whiteness,
Yet, earthward stooping, wears an earthly glow.
　Mysteries the Muse would hide, the Bards reveal —
They love to wound; her mission is to heal.

# SONG

Sing the old song, amid the sounds dispersing
   That burden treasured in your hearts too long;
      Sing it, with voice low-breathed, but never name
        her:
She will not hear you, in her turrets nursing
 · High thoughts, too high to mate with mortal song —
      Bend o'er her, gentle Heaven, but do not claim
        her!


In twilight caves, and secret lonelinesses,
   She shades the bloom of her unearthly days;
      And the soft winds alone have power to woo
        her:
Far off we catch the dark gleam of her tresses;
      And wild birds haunt the wood-walks where she
        strays,   ·
      Intelligible music warbling to her.


That Spirit charged to follow and defend her, —
   He also, doubtless, suffers this love-pain;
      And she, perhaps, is sad, hearing his sighing:
And yet that face is not so sad as tender;
      Like some sweet singer's, when her sweetest strain
        From the heaved heart is gradually dying!

## TO ——

My hope, in happier days than these,
　　My love — hope past;
Memory's one star on lonely seas;
　　My anchor, last!
Why ask'st thou, with subdued surprise,
　　And that mild glee,
Wherefore I turn, still turn mine eyes
　　From all, to thee?

The blind man turns — and none forbids —
　　Into sunshine
His filmy, cold, unlighted lids;
　　The deaf incline
To harps whence songs, for them unborn,
　　Float light and free;
To graves long-cherished, hearts forlorn;
　　And I to thee.

## AN OLD POET'S LOVE

### I

AH, that a lightly-lifted hand
　Should thus man's soul depress or raise,
And wield, as with a magic wand,
　A spirit steeled in earlier days!

Ah, that a voice whose speech is song,
    Whose pathos weeps, whose gladness smiles,
Should melt a heart unmoved so long,
    And charm it to the Syren Isles!

Ah, that one presence, morn or eve,
    Should fill deserted halls with light;
One breeze-like step, departing, leave
    The noonday darker than the night!

Thy power is great: but Love and Youth
    Conspire with thee.   With thee they dwell:
From those kind eyes, in tenderest ruth,
    On mine they look, and say, — "Farewell!"


## II

As when, deep chaunts abruptly stayed,
    The Thoughts that, music-born, advanced
In tides of puissance, music-swayed,
    And waves that in the glory danced, —

Contract, subside, and leave at last,
    Where late the abounding floods were spread,
A vale of darkness, grim and vast,
    A buried river's rocky bed;

Thus — when thou goest — my heart, my life
    Descend to dim sepulchral caves;
My world, but late with rapture rife,
    Becomes a world of rocks and graves.

Come back!   From mountain-cells, afar,
   My soul's strong river shall return.
Come back!   Again the Morning Star
   Shall shine against the exhaustless urn.


### III

" Can Love be just? can Hope be wise?
   Can Youth renew his honours dead? "
On me my Psyche turned her eyes;
   And all my great resolves were fled.

"Psyche," I said, "when thou art nigh
   Transpicuous grow the mists of years;
I cannot ever wholly die
   If on my grave should drop thy tears.

"Nor thine a part in mortal hours;
   Thy flower nor autumn knows, nor May;
Thou bendest from sidereal bowers,
   A dateless glory, fresh for aye!

"Though I be nothing, yet the best
   To thee no gift of price could give;
Fall then, in radiance, on my breast,
   And in thy blessing bid me live!"

## TROUVÈRE SONGS

### I

I MAKE not songs, but only find;
   Love, following still the circling sun,
His carol casts on every wind,
   And other singer is there none.

I follow Love, though far he flies;
   I sing his song, at random found
Like plume some bird of Paradise
   Drops, passing, on our dusky bound.

In some, methinks, at times there glows
   The passion of some heavenlier sphere:
These too I sing; but sweetest those
   I dare not sing, and faintly hear.

### II

Phœbus paced the wooded mountains,
   Kindled dawn, and met a doe;
"Child, what ails thee that thou rovest
   O'er my bright hills, sad and slow?

"That upon thy left side only
   Thou thy noontide sleep dost take;
That thy foot the fountain troubles
   Ever, ere thy thirst thou slake?"

T

Answered thus the weeping creature:
  "Once beside me raced a fawn;
Seest her, O thou God all-seeing!
  O'er thy hills, in wood or lawn?

"On my left side sleep I only,
  For 'tis there my anguish stirs;
And my foot the fountain troubles,
  Lest it yield me shape like hers."

Then the Sun-God marvelled, musing,—
  "When my foolish Daphne died,
Rooted 'mid Peneian laurels,
  Scarce one little hour I sighed."

## PEASANT'S SONG

HARK, the Spring!  She calls!
  With a thousand voices
'Mid the echoing forest-halls
  One great heart rejoices!

Hills, where young lambs bound,
  Whiten o'er with daisies;
Flag-flowers light the lower ground,
  Where the old steer grazes.

Meadows laugh, flower-gay;
   Every breeze that passes
Waves the seed-cloud's gleaming grey
   O'er the greener grasses.

O thou Spring! be strong,
   Exquisite new-comer!
And the onset baffle long
   Of advancing Summer!

## ZARA TO ANTAR

I HEARD his voice, and I was dumb
   Because to his my spirit cleaved.
He called me from afar: I come.
   Because I loved him, I believed.

He said, "Though love be secret yet,
   Eternity its truth shall prove."
It seemed not gift, but ancient debt
   Discharged, to answer love with love.

## MARRIAGE SONG

LOVE begins upon the heights,
   As on tree-tops in the spring
April with green foot alights
   While the birds are carolling:

Ay, but April ends with May,—
Love must have the marriage-day!

Love begins upon the heights,
    As o'er snowy summits sail
First the dewy matin lights
    Destined soon to reach the vale:
Ay, but maidens must not grieve
That morn of love hath noon and eve.

Love is Dream and Vision first;
    Proud young Love the earth disdains;
But his cold streams, mountain-nursed,
    Warm them in the fruitful plains
Ere the marriage-day is sped:
Peal the bells!   The bride is wed!

## SONG

SEEK not the tree of silkiest bark
    And balmiest bud
To carve her name, while yet 'tis dark,
    Upon the wood!
The world is full of noble tasks,
    And wreaths hard-won;
Each work demands strong hearts, strong hands,
    Till day is done.

Sing not that violet-veinèd skin,
   That cheek's pale roses;
The lily of that form wherein
   Her soul reposes!
Forth to the fight, true man, true knight!
   The clash of arms
Shall more prevail than whispered tale
   To win her charms.


The warrior for the True, the Right,
   Fights in Love's name;
The love that lures thee from that fight
   Lures thee to shame.
That love which lifts the heart, yet leaves
   The spirit free,—
That love, or none, is fit for one,
   Man-shaped, like thee.


## LINES

Heart-wingèd once; self-doomed
   To pine in bonds the saddest;
Strong spirit, self-entombed
   Within the vaults thou madest:
Thy Will it is, thy Will
   That holds thee prisoner still!

O Soul, in vain thou strainest
Against thy prison bar;
Of all vain things the vainest
Our poor, half efforts are.
Wholly be free! — till then
Thou dost but hug thy chain.


## A LAMENT

A sigh in the morning grey!
And a solitary tear,
Slow to gather, slow to fall;
And a painful flush of shame
At the naming of thy name —
This is little, this is all,
False one, which remains to say
That thy love of old was here;
That thy love hath passed away!

## "THEY NEVER MET"

SOMEWHERE she lives — I know not who or where —
  The good, the kind, the tender, and the true,
  Whose least of charms is this, that she is fair;
Who lives unknown, scarce known, or known to few.
He will not meet her! her, who might renew
  A spring that flowerless died, and bid him wear
  That summer crown they only win who share —
Noon's forest-wreath, still fresh with morning dew.

Is she then happy?  Are her fates fulfilled?
  Perchance she sits, this fading eve, alone
  By yonder ebbing Thames, with fingers chilled,
Clasping some rain-washed rosebud never blown.
  How oft he may have passed thee, sweet Unknown,
  Sole amid crowds, with pulse a moment stilled !


## TO ——

### I

SHE sat amid a soft-eyed company
  Of little children, whom she taught to love
  That God Who deigned a child on earth to move,—
And, loving Him, to fear.  Hand, lip, and eye,
And many a smile, and sometimes a short sigh,
  Were beautiful to incite and to reprove;
  And with that holier wisdom from above
Enlarge our sorrowful humanity.

And yet, O blameless, and thyself a child!
   How canst thou teach?  Thy rosy lips make sweet
   The faults they fain would chide!  Of all that group
The timidest such wrath as thine would meet
   Gladly, if so that dovelike hand might droop
   Upon her shoulder or her tresses wild.

II

Happy are they who kiss thee, morn and even,
   Parting the hair upon thy forehead white!
   For them the sky is bluer and more bright,
And purer their thanksgivings rise to Heaven.
Happy are they to whom thy songs are given;
   Happy are they on whom thy hands alight;
   And happiest they for whom thy prayers at night
In tender piety so oft have striven!

Away with vain regrets and selfish sighs —
   Even I, dear friend, am lonely, not unblest;
   Permitted sometimes on that form to gaze,
Or feel the light of those consoling eyes;
   If but a moment on my cheek it stays,
   I know that gentle beam from all the rest!

III

The spring of my sweet life thou madest thine;
   And on my summer glories thou hast fed;
   And now the vernal melodies are dead

On lips that mourn for joys no longer mine.
The summer brilliance now hath ceased to shine
 Upon a brow so oft disquieted
 By agonising doubts; thy love is fled;
And thou art flying — how dare I repine?

How could I hope so great a love would cleave
 To one whose fault too well was known to thee?
 Lament not, O my love; or, if thou grieve,
For me lament not, though my grief thou share;
 For I have known in dreams my destiny,
 And what I ought to welcome I can bear.


IV


Let me be near thee, and I will not touch
 Thy hand; or grieve thee with reproach or praise;
 Or look into thine eyes. Is this too much?
Sweet Lady, say not so, for I would gaze
On thee for ever. Be but what thou art,
 A Beauty shrined within a silver haze;
 And in the silence let me fill my heart
With memories calmly stored for wintry days.

O Lady! there is sorrow here below;
 And gladness seldom comes, and cannot last;
 Thou art all summer; thou wilt never know
The cold and cloudy skies which I forecast;
 Deny not thou long years of future woe
 Their comfort sad and sole — a happy Past.

### V

Pause, lovely Lady, pause! with downward eye
  Regard this humble tomb awhile; and read
  The name of him who loved you well, now freed
From pains of love — ah, mournful liberty!
Sigh forth, too late, an unavailing sigh;
  And, if thy spirit be to pity moved,
  Pray that a ceaseless dream of her he loved
Abide upon him everlastingly.

Stay, lovely Lady, stay!   O, stay for hours!
  I feel thy tear-drops falling one by one.
  Yet do not stay, for grief and shame it were
That tears should fall so fast from eyes so fair;
  And feet, that scarcely bend the meadow flowers,
  Linger so long upon the chilling stone.


## TO AN INFANT

FAMILIAR Spirit! that so graciously
  Dost take whatever fortune may befall,
  Trusting thy fragile form to the arms of all,
And never counting it indignity
To sit caressed upon the humblest knee;
  Thou, having yet no words, aloud dost call
  Upon our hearts; the fever and the gall
Of our dark bosoms are reproved in thee.

From selfish fears and lawless wishes free,
  Thou hast no painful feeling of thy weakness;
  From shafts malign and pride's base agony
Protected by the pillows of thy meekness;
  Thou hast thy little loves which do not grieve
    thee,
  Unquiet make thee, or unhappy leave thee.

## HUMAN LIFE

SAD is our youth, for it is ever going,
  Crumbling away beneath our very feet;
  Sad is our life, for onward it is flowing,
In current unperceived, because so fleet;
Sad are our hopes, for they were sweet in sowing,
  But tares, self-sown, have overtopped the wheat:
  Sad are our joys, for they were sweet in blowing;
And still, O still, their dying breath is sweet!

And sweet is youth, although it hath bereft us
  Of that which made our childhood sweeter still;
  And sweet our life's decline, for it hath left us
A nearer Good to cure an older Ill;
  And sweet are all things, when we learn to prize
    them
  Not for their sake, but His, Who grants them or
    denies them.

## ÆSCHYLUS

A sea-cliff carved into a bas-relief!
  Dark thoughts and sad, conceived by brooding
      Nature,
  Brought forth in storm: — dread shapes of Titan
      stature,
Emblems of Fate and Change, Revenge and Grief,
And Death and Life: — a caverned Hieroglyph
  Confronting still, with thunder-blasted frieze,
  All stress of years, and winds, and wasting seas: —
The stranger nears it in his fragile skiff,

And hides his eyes.   Few, few shall pass, great
      Bard,
  Thy dim sea-portals!   Entering, fewer yet
  Shall pierce thy mystic meanings, deep and hard;
But these shall owe to thee an endless debt;
  The Eleusinian caverns they shall tread
  That wind beneath man's heart; and wisdom learn,
      with dread.

## TASSO'S HOUSE AT SORRENTO

O Leonora, here thy Tasso dwelt,
  Secure, ere yet thy beauty he had seen;
  Here with bright face, and unterrestrial mien,
He walked, ere yet thy shadow he had felt;
From that green rock he watched the sunset melt

On through the waves; yon cavern was his screen
    When first those hills, which gird the glowing scene,
Were thronged with heavenly warriors, and he knelt

To hail the vision!   Syren baths to him
    Were nothing; Pagan grot, or classic fane,
    Or glistening pavement, seen through billows dim;
Far, far o'er these he gazed on Judah's plain,
    And more than manhood wrought was in the boy —
    Why did the Stranger meddle in his joy?


## THE RENAISSANCE AND SAVONAROLA

I

PAINTER, that on these sacred convent walls
    The symbols paintest of the fleeting Hours,
    Reserve thine art, poor spoil from Pagan bowers,
To deck withal the rich man's secular halls!
Are these the Hours? aerial Bacchanals,
    With urn down-bent, or basket heaped with flowers,
    Through sunshine borne, light Zephyr's paramours?—
Thralls though we be, we are not Pleasure's thralls!

When God, with thunder, and his prophet's voice,
    The temples where of old he chose to dwell
    Chooses to shake in judgment, cleanse or quell,
How impious sounds thy summons to rejoice!
    Erase thy work; kneel on the tombstones bare;
    Thine eye with fastings purge; make firm thy hand
        with prayer!

## II

Then rise, and paint the Hours; and launch them forth
  Like sequent arrows hurled from God's right hand,
  Or eagles of the ocean borne to earth
By solid storm their wings no more withstand;
Yet, calm in speed, a stern, predestined band,
  In meditative might or gloomy mirth
  Speed them, dread forms of elemental birth;
And let one bear the trump, and one the brand!

Fix thou their mighty eyes the dark locks under
  Massed o'er their fervid foreheads, like a cloud
  Whose heart is flame; and be their faces bowed,
As though they listened to unsleeping thunder;
  The breaking of the billows of Time's sea
  On the far confines of Eternity!

## GALATEA AND URANIA; OR, ART AND FAITH

"DREAD, venerable Goddess, whom I fear,
  Gaze not upon me from thy starry height!
  I fear thy levelled shafts of ruthless light,
Thine unfamiliar radiance and severe.
Thy sceptre bends not! stern, defined, and clear,
  Thy Laws; thy face intolerantly bright;
  Thine is the empire of the Ruled and Right;
Never hadst thou a part in smile or tear!

" I love the curving of the wind-arched billow ;
 The dying flute tone, sweeter for its dying;
 To me less dear the Pine tree than the Willow,
The mountain than the shadows o'er it flying."
 Thus Galatea sang — whilst o'er the waters
 Urania leant — and cowered 'mid Ocean's foam-
  white daughters.


## THE POET'S SONG

FAR rather let us loathe and scorn the power
 Of Song, than seek her fane with hearts impure,
 Panting for praise or pay, the vulgar lure
Of those on whom the Muse doth scantly shower,
Or not at all, her amaranthine dower;
 Ye that would serve her, first of this be sure,
 Her glorious Pæans will for aye endure
Whether or not she smile upon your bower.

Go forth, Eternal Melodies, go forth
 O'er all the world, and in your broad arms wind
  it!
 Go forth, as ye are wont, from South to North;
No spot so barren but your spells can find it.
 So long as Heaven is vaulted o'er the earth,
 So long your power survives, and who can bind
  it?

## SOLITUDE WITHOUT VOCATION

In this Seclusion, from the world secure,
   Her frauds, her force, her clamour, and her din,
   O, what a prosperous height might virtue win,
If, entering first these courts, the soul were pure!
But to a tainted soul, how weak the lure
   Of outward things compared with snares within,
   Where thought tracks thought, insatiable pursuer,
On through the inmost caves of lurking sin —

Dark thoughts which nobler presences had scared,
   And palpable duties crushed!   Ah, well of old
Fabled the priest, if priest he were or bard,
His Dian strenuous of life and bold;
   A Huntress o'er the mountain summits hard,
   Her couch beside the fountain calm but cold.

## A POET TO A PAINTER

That which my fault has made me, O paint not!
   Paint me as that which I desire to be:
   The unaccomplished good that died in thought,
That Limbo of high hopes, seek out, set free,
And all I might have been concede to me;
   The mask my errors and the world have wrought,
   Remove; the cloud disperse; erase the blot;
Bid from my brow the temporal darkness flee!

In that celestial and pure fount, whereof
Some drops affused my childhood, bathe me
wholly;
And shield me from my own deserts; lest they,
Who now but see me by the light of love,
A sterner insight learn from thee one day;
And love pass from them like some outworn
folly.


## THE POET'S CHOICE

FREE born, it is my purpose to die free.
Away, degrading cares; and ye, not less,
Delights of sense, and gauds of worldliness!
I have no part in you, nor you in me.
They that walk brave, wear the world's livery;
Their badge of service is their sumptuous dress;
Seek then your prey in gilded palaces;
Revere my hovel's humble liberty!

Are there no flowers on earth, in heaven no stars,
That we must place in such low things our
trust?
Let me have noble toils, if toil I must,
The Patriot's task, or Friendship's sacred cares!
Beside my board that man shall break no crust,
Who sells his birthright for a feast of dust.

U

## ON READING AN UNTRUE CHARGE

BEAUTIFUL Land!   They said, "He loves thee not!"
  But in a churchyard, 'mid thy meadows, lie
  The bones of no disloyal ancestry,                     •
To whom in me disloyal were the thought
Which wronged thee.   For my youth thy Shakspeare
          wrought;
  For me thy minsters raised their towers on high;
  Thou gav'st me friends whose memory cannot die:—
I love thee, and for that cause left unsought

Thy praise.   Thy ruined cloisters, forests green,
  Thy moors where still the branching wild deer roves,
  Dear haunts of mine by sun and moon have been
From Cumbrian peaks to Devon's laughing coves.
  They love thee less, fair Land, who ne'er had heart
  To take, for truth's sake, 'gainst thyself thy part.


## POLAND AND RUSSIA

THE Strong One with the Weak One reasons thus:
  "Through sin of thine our eagle wings are clipt;
  Through frost of thine our summer branch is nipt;
Thy wounds accuse; thy rags are mutinous;
The nations note thine aspect dolorous,
  Like some starved shape that cowers in charnel crypt,
  Or landscape in eclipse perpetual dipt,
And, ignorant, cavil, not at thee but us!"

Then answer makes that worn voice, stern and
    slow:
  "Am I a dog the scourger's hand that licks,
  And fattens? Blind reproof but spurns the
    pricks.
That which I am thou mad'st me! long ago
  My face thou grav'dst to be a face of woe,
  Fixed as the fixed face of a Crucifix."

## ISLAM

THAT Asian ardour, deep, and wide, and still,
  Which once, like Heaven o'er glowing sands, did
    brood
  Over this People's heart, stubborn and rude,
Hath left them. Did it yet their pulses fill,
They had not lost that fateful might of Will
  Which from Imaus on to Atlas hewed
  A way before them — in its terrible mood
"Making ridiculous" the boasted skill

Of Western Art alike and Arms. Of old
  This People's spirit was an arch of fire,
  Like a "clear heat at harvest." Now remains
Nought but the hoary herb and branded plains,
  Which beasts shall trample, issuing in their ire
  Forth from the depth of their morasses cold!

## THE AMERICAN STRUGGLE

SWORD! ere the sheath that hid thy light so long
  That splendour quench, go thou like lightning
      forth,
  High Bride of Justice, not of South or North,
And raise, as now, the weak, and quell the strong!
Advance, till from the black man's hearth the song
  Rises to God, and by the black man's hearth
  Humanity hath leave in godly mirth
To sit, forgetful of her ancient wrong!

Then rest for ever; for to work like thine,
  While the world lasts, no other can succeed
  Equal, or second.   Hang in heaven, a Sign,
But stoop no more to earth or earthly need;
  Nor ever leave thy starry home august,
  Vassal of vulgar wars, and prone Ambition's lust.

## ON THE CENTENARY OF AMERICAN
## LIBERTY

A CENTURY of sunrises hath bowed
  Its fulgent forehead 'neath the ocean-floor
  Since first upon the West's astonished shore,
Like some huge Alp, forth struggling through the
      cloud,

A new-born nation stood, to Freedom vowed.
 Within that time how many an Empire hoar,
 And young Republic, flushed with wealth and war,
Alike have changed the ermine for the shroud!

O "sprung from earth's first blood," O tempest-
  nursed,
 For thee what Fates? — I know not. This I know:
 The Soul's great freedom — gift, of gifts the
  first —
Thou first on man in fulness didst bestow;
 Hunted elsewhere, God's Church with thee found
  rest:
 Thy future's Hope is She — that queenly Guest.


## EPIGRAMS

### I

#### A FAREWELL

Round me thy great woods sigh
In their full-foliaged glory; but I die.
 Ah, blame me not; although
Tired and o'er-spent, I never prayed to go.
 In thine old towers I leave
A cradled pledge to take his mother's part,—
 To vex thee not, nor grieve,
Yet lay, at times, my hand about thy heart.

## II

### AN EPITAPH

FROM Youth's soft haunt she passed to Love's fair nest;
Thence on to larger Love and heavenlier rest:
Four years their sunshine, two their shadows lent
To enrich a heart with either lot content.
Pray well, pure Spirit! and some sad grace accord
To him once more thy suppliant; once thy lord.

## III

### THREE PRAYERS

THREE prayers to Heaven the Lover doth present:
That she he loves rest ever innocent:
Next for her happiness: and last that he
Shield of that goodness and that peace may be.
Dear friend, repine no longer — be content;
For thou hast gained two wishes out of three!

## IV

### A TRAVELLER'S GRACE

TAKE, pretty birds — to you these crumbs are given —
   Your portion of our meal ere yet begun;
And wait our thanks in melody to Heaven,
   Should we forget them, when that meal is done.

## V

### ON A GREAT PLAGIARIST

PHŒBUS drew back with just disdain
    The wreath; the Delphic Temple frowned.
The suppliant fled to Hermes' fane,
    That stood on lower, wealthier ground.

The Thief-God spake, with smile star-bright:
    "Go thou where luckier poets browse
The pastures of the Lord of Light,
    And do — what I did with his cows."

## VI

### AN EPICUREAN'S EPITAPH

WHEN from my lips the last faint sigh is blown
    By Death, dark waver of Lethean plumes,
O, press not then with monumental stone
    This forehead smooth, nor weigh me down with
        glooms
        From green bowers, grey with dew,
        Of Rosemary and Rue!
Choose for my bed some bath of sculptured marble
    Wreathed with gay nymphs; and lay me — not
        alone —
Where sunbeams fall, flowers wave, and light birds
        warble,
    To those who loved me, murmuring in soft tone, —

"Here lies our friend, from pain secure and cold;
And spreads his limbs in peace under the sun-warmed
      mould!"

## VII

### AN EPITAPH WITHOUT A NAME

I HAD a Name.   A wreath of woven air,
  A wreath of letters blended, none knew why,
Floated, a vocal phantom, here and there,
    For one brief season, like the dragon-fly
      That flecks the noontide beam,
Flickering o'er downward, forest-darkened stream.
What word those Letters shaped I tell you not:
Wherefore should such this maiden marble blot,
Faint echo, last and least, of foolish Fame? —
I am a Soul; nor care to have a Name.

## VIII

### DE VIA

FROM North unto South, from the East unto the West
      There is no rest;
Wind sigheth unto wind, sea moaneth unto sea,
      "Not in me,"
  And the loud waves that roar
  In the deep, and on the shore: —
Never, till thou resteth in the green earth's breast,
      Shalt thou rest.

# MEMORIAL POEMS

An altar I would rear beside the Rhine,
    And by the Arno, and the Adrian sea,
    For there, O Friends beloved, one hour had we,
And thence, O Friends beloved and ever mine,
We ranged together.   Alp and Apennine
    Henceforth are rich in household nooks to me,
    Nor wholly solitary can I be
Whether the Palm my tent I make, or Pine.

How large a portion of earth's populous ball
    Have you to me endeared!   Therefore, less keen
    Sorrow one day shall prove, or Fortune's spleen,
Or all the ills that lonely age befall.
    Ah yes ; — and yet, had I been worthier, all
    Which was so dear still dearer might have been.

# CHRISTMAS, 1860

## I

Alone, among thy books, once more I sit;
  No sound there stirs, except the flapping fire;
  Strange shadows of old times about me flit,
As sinks the midnight lamp, or flickers higher.
I see thee pace the room; with eye thought-lit
  Back, back, thou com'st once more to my desire;
  Low-toned thou read'st, once more, the verse new-
      writ,—
Too deep, too pure for worldlings to admire.


That brow all honour, that all-gracious hand,
  That cordial smile, and clear voice musical,
  That noble bearing, mien of high command,
Yet void of pride — to-night I have them all.
  Ah, phantoms vain of thought!  The Christmas air
  Is white with flying flakes.  Where art thou—where?


## II

To-night, upon thy roof the snows are lying;
  The Christmas snows lie heavy on thy trees;
  A dying dirge, that soothes the year in dying,
Swells from thy woodlands on the midnight breeze.

Our loss is ancient; many a heart is sighing
　　This night a late one, or by slow degrees
　　Heals some old wound, to God's high grace reply-
　　　　ing : —
A time there was when thou wert like to these.

Where art thou?　In what unimagined sphere
　　Liv'st thou, sojourner, or no transient guest?
　　By whom companioned?　Access hath she near,
In life thy nearest, and beloved the best?
　　What memory hast thou of thy loved ones here?
　　Hangs the great Vision o'er thy place of rest?


### III

"Sweet-sounding bells, blithe summoners to prayer!"
　　The answer man can yield not, ye bestow;
　　Your answer is a little Infant bare,
Wafted to earth on night-winds whispering low.
Blow him to Bethlehem, airs angelic, blow!
　　There doth the Mother-maid his couch prepare.
　　His harbour is her bosom!　Drop him there,
Soft as a snow-flake on a bank of snow.

Sole Hope of man!　Sole Hope for us, for thee!
　　"To us a Prince is given: a Child is born!"
　　*Thou* sang'st of Bethlehem, and of Calvary,
The Maid Immaculate and the twisted Thorn.
　　Where'er thou art, not far, not far is He
　　Whose banner whitens in yon Christmas morn!

# AT VEVEY

### SEPTEMBER 15, 1856

FROM terraced heights that rise in ranks
  Thick set with almond, fig, and maize,
O'er waters blue as violet banks,
  I hear the songs of boyhood's days.

Up walnut slopes, at morn and eve,
  And downward o'er the pearly shore
From Clarens on they creep; nor leave
  Uncheered cold Chillon's dungeon-floor.

Fair girls that please a mother's pride,
  Bright boys from joy of heart that sing,
The voice of bridegroom and of bride,—
  Through clustered vines how clear they ring!

For me, they blot these southern bowers;
  The ghosts of years gone by they wake;
They send the drift of northern showers
  Low-whispering o'er a narrower lake.

Once more upon the couch he lies
  Who ruled his halls with stately cheer;
Waves slow the lifted hand; with eyes
  And lips rewards the strains most dear.

And ah! from yon empurpled slope
　　What fragrance swells that arch beneath!
Geranium, jasmine, heliotrope —
　　They stay my breath : of her they breathe!

Flower-lover! wheresoe'er thou art,
　　May flowers and sunshine greet thee still,
And voices vocal to the heart:
　　No sound approach of sad or ill!

## SIR WILLIAM ROWAN HAMILTON

### I

FRIEND of past years, the holy and the blest,
　　When all my day shone out, a long sunrise;
　　When aspirations seemed but sympathies,
In such familiar nearness were they dressed;
When Song, with swan-like plumes and starry crest,
　　O'er-circled earth and beat against the skies,
　　And fearless Science raised her reverent eyes
From heaven to heaven, that each its God confessed

With homage ever widening!　Friend beloved!
　　From me those days are passed; yet still, O, still,
　　This night my heart with influx strange they fill
Of beaming memories from my vanished youth:
　　On thee — the temporal veil by Death removed —
　　Rests the great Vision of Eternal Truth!

## II

At times I see that ample forehead lit,
  Bright as the day-spring round the mounted lark;
  At times I see thee stand in musing fit;
At times in woodlands of that twilight park,
Deciphering well-loved names on beechen bark;
  Where Rotha's moonlight ripples past thee flit,
  I see thee kiss a grave — then by it sit —
Her grave that left the land's chief Poet dark.

This day I read thy letters.   Word and scene
  Recur with strangely mingled joy and ruth;
  Thy soul translucent; yet thine insight keen,
Thy heart's deep yearnings and perpetual youth;
  Thy courtesy, thy reverence, and thy truth —
  All that thou wert, and all thou mightst have been!


### EDWIN, EARL OF DUNRAVEN

Once more I pace thy pillared halls,
  And hear the organ echoes sigh
In blissful death on storied walls:
  But where art thou? not here; nor nigh.

Once more the rapt spring-breezes send
  A flash o'er yonder winding flood,
And with the garden's fragrance blend
  A fresher breath from lawn and wood.

Friend! where art thou?   Thy works reply;
   The lowly School; the high-arched Fane.
Who loves his kind can never die;
   Who serves his God, with God shall reign.

## SIR JOHN SIMEON

### FEAST OF THE PURIFICATION

### I

THIS day we keep our Candlemas in snow.
   Wan is the sky; a bitter wind, and drear,
   Wrinkles the bosom of yon blackening mere;
Of these I reck not, but of thee, and O!
Of that bright Roman morn, so long ago,
   When, children new of her, that Church more
      dear
   To liegeful hearts with each injurious year,
We watched the famed Procession circling slow.

Once more I see it wind with lights upholden
   On through the Sistine, on and far away;
   Once more I mark beneath its radiance golden
Thy forehead shine, and, with it kindling, say,—
   " Rehearsals dim were those, O friend; this hour
   Surely God's light it is that on thee rests in power!"

## II

Again we met.   We trod the fields and farms
  Of that fair isle, thy happy English home;
  We gazed upon blue sea, and snowy foam,
Clipt in the jutting headland's woody arms.
The year had reached the fulness of her charms;
  The Church's year, from strength to strength in-
      creased,
  Its zenith held, that great Assumption feast
Whose sun with annual joy the whole earth warms.

That day how swiftly rushed from thy full heart
  Hope's glorying flood!   How high thy fancy soared,
  Kenning, though far, once more thine England's
      crest,
A light to Christendom's old heaven restored!
  "In a large room" thy heart its home had found:
  The land we trod that day to thee was holy ground.


## III

The world external knew thee but in part;
  It saw and honoured what was least in thee:
  The loyal trust, the inborn courtesy;
The ways so winning, yet so pure from art;
The cordial reverence, keen to all desert,
  All save thine own; the accost so frank and free;
  The public zeal that toiled, but not for fee,
And shunned alike base praise and hireling's mart.
    X

These things men saw; but, deeper far than these,
   The under-current of thy soul worked on,
   Unvexed by surface-ripple, beam, or breeze,
And, unbeheld, its way to ocean won.
   Life of thy life was still that Christian Faith
   The sophist scorns.    It failed thee not in death.


## CARDINAL NEWMAN

THY ninety years on earth have passed away.
   At last thou restest 'mid that heavenly clime
   Where Act is Rest, and Age perpetual prime;
Thy noblest, holiest work begins this day,—
Begins, not ends!    Best Work is Prayer; and they
   Who plead, absolved from bonds of Space and
      Time,
   With lordliest labour work that work sublime,
Order our planet with benignest sway.


So work, great Spirit!    Thy toils foregone, each year,
   Bear fruit on earth!    Thousands but praise thee
      now;
   Those laureates soon will bend a brightening brow
O'er tomes of thine; on each may drop a tear
   For friends that o'er blind oceans pushed their
      prow,
   Self-cheated of a guiding light so clear.

## CARDINAL MANNING

I LEARNED his greatness first at Lavington.
  The moon had early sought her bed of brine,
  But we discoursed till now each starry sign
Had sunk; our theme was one, and one alone.
"Two minds supreme," he said, "our earth has
      known;
  One sang in science; one served God in song;
  Aquinas — Dante." Slowly in me grew strong
A thought, — "These two great minds in him are
      one; —

"'Lord, what shall this man do?'" Later, at Rome,
  Beside the dust of Peter and of Paul,
  Eight hundred mitred sires of Christendom
In Council sat. I marked him 'mid them all;
  I thought of that long night in years gone by,
  And cried, — "At last, my question meets reply."

## ROBERT BROWNING

SHAKESPEARE'S old oak "gnarled and unwedgeable"
  Yields not so sweet a wood to harp or lyre
  As tree of smoother grain; and chorded shell
Is spanned by strings tenderer than iron wire.
What then? Stern tasks iron and oak require!
  Iron deep-mined, hard oak from stormy fell;

Steel-armed, the "black ship" breasts the ocean's
       swell;
Oak-ribbed, laughs back the raging tempest's ire.

Old friend, thy song I deem a ship whose hold
    Is stored with mental spoils of ampler price
    Than Spain's huge galleons, in her age of gold,
Or Indian caracks from the isles of spice.
    Brave Argosy! cleave long the waves as now;
    And all the Sea-Gods sing around thy prow!

## ALFRED TENNYSON

### I

#### THE LAND'S VIGIL

How many a face throughout the Imperial Isle,
    From Kentish shores to Scottish hill or hall,
    From Cambrian vales to Windsor's royal pile,
Turned sadly towards one House more sad than all,—
Turned day by day, fear-blanched! When evening's
       pall
    Shrouded a day that scarce had heart to smile,
    How oft sad eyes, spelled by one thought the while,
Not seeing, seemed to see a taper small,

Night after night, flashed from one casement high!
    Let these men sing his praise! Others there are
    Who fitlier might have sung them in old time,

Since they loved best who loved him in his prime.
  Their youth, and his, expired long since and far.
  Now he is gone, it seems "again to die."

## II

### WESTMINSTER ABBEY

'Tis well!  Not always nations are ingrate!
  He gave his country "of his best; " and she
  Gave to her bard in glorious rivalry
Her whole great heart.    A People and a State
Had met, through love a tomb to consecrate.
  In the Abbey old each order and degree
  Low knelt, and upward gazing seemed to see,
Not that dark vault, but Heaven's expanding gate.

O'er him the death-song he had made they sung: —
  Thus, when in Rome the Prince of Painters died,
  His Art's last marvel o'er his bier was hung,
At once in heavenly hope and honest pride:
  Thus England honoured him she loved that day;
  Thus many prayed — as England's Saints will pray.

## III

### THE POET

None sang of Love more nobly; few as well;
  Of Friendship none with pathos so profound;
  Of Duty sternliest-proved when myrtle-crowned;
Of English grove and rivulet, mead and dell;
Great Arthur's Legend he alone dared tell;

Milton and Dryden feared to tread that ground;
For him alone o'er Camelot's faery bound
The "horns of Elf-land" blew their magic spell.

Since Shakespeare and since Wordsworth none hath
    sung
  So well his England's greatness; none hath given
  Reproof more fearless or advice more sage.
None inlier taught how near to earth is Heaven;
  With what vast concords Nature's harp is strung;
  How base false pride; faction's fanatic rage.

## IV

### THE REWARD

The land, whose loveliness in verse of thine
  Shows lovelier yet than prank'd on Nature's page,
  Shall prove thy poet in some future age,
Sing thee, her Poet, not in measured line
Or metric stave, but music more benign;
  Shall point to British Galahads who wage
  Battle on Wrong; to British maids who gage,
Like Agnes, heart and hope to Love divine.

Worn men, like thy Ulysses, scorning fear,
  Shall tempt strange seas beneath an alien star;
  Old men, from cherished haunts and households
    dear
Summoned by death to realms unknown and far,
  Thy "Silent Voices" from on high shall hear,—
  With happier auspice cross thy "harbour bar."